Wilson's PRESERVED STEAM RAILWAYS Timetable

Argus Books

ARGUS BOOKS
Argus House
Boundary Way
Hemel Hempstead
Herts HP2 7ST
England

First published by Argus Books 1992

ISBN 1 85486 075 5

Frontispiece Photograph
DAME VERA storms the last few yards
of the notorious 1 in 49 Goathland Bank
at the North Yorkshire Moors Railway.
Photo by C.D.Wilson

Design & Phototypesetting by Albion Design, Whitstable
Printed & bound in Great Britain by Clays Ltd, St Ives PLC, Bungay, Suffolk.

Alphabetical Table of Listed Sites

Alderney Railway Society
Alford Valley Railway
Amberley Chalk Pits Museum
Avon Valley Railway
Ayrshire Railway Pres. Society
Bala Lake Railway
Beamish Open Air Museum
Bluebell Railway
Bodmin & Wenford Railway
Bo'ness & Kinneil Railway
Bowes Railway
Brecon Mountain Railway
Bressingham Steam Museum
Bristol Harbour Railway
Buckinghamshire Railway Centre
Bure Valley Railway
Cadeby Light Railway
Caledonian Railway
Chasewater Light Railway
Chatterly Whitfield Mining Museum
Chinnor & Princes Risborough Railway
Cholsey & Wallingford Railway
Cleethorpes Coast Light Railway
Colne Valley Railway
Coventry Steam Railway Centre
Crewe Heritage Centre
Darlington Railway Museum
Dean Forest Railway
Didcot Railway Centre
East Anglian Railway Museum
East Lancashire Railway
East Somerset Railway
Embsay Steam Railway
Fairbourne Railway
Ffestiniog Railway
Forest Railroad Park
Foxfield Light Railway
Gloucester & Warwickshire Railway
Great Central Railway
Groudle Glen Railway
Gwili Railway
Hunsbury Hill Industrial Museum
Isfield Steam Railway
Isle of Man Railway
Isle of Mull Railway
Isle of Wight Railway
Keighley & Worth Valley Railway
Kent & East Sussex Railway

Kirklees Light Railway
Lakeside & Haverthwaite Railway
Launceston Steam Railway
Leighton Buzzard Railway
Llanberis Lake Railway
Llangollen Railway
Lochty Private Railway
Mangapps Farm Museum
Market Bosworth Light Railway
Middleton Railway
Mid-Hants Railway
Midland Railway Centre
Moors Valley Railway
National Railway Museum
Nene Valley Railway
North Downs Steam Railway
North Norfolk Railway
North Staffordshire Railway
North Yorkshire Moors Railway
Paignton & Dartmouth Railway
Peak Rail
Plym Valley Railway
Pontypool & Blaenavon Railway
Ravenglass & Eskdale Railway
Romney, Hythe & Dymchurch Railway
Rutland Railway Museum
Severn Valley Railway
Sittingbourne & Kemsley Light Railway
Snowdon Mountain Railway
South Devon Railway
Southport Railway Centre
South Tynedale Railway
Steamtown (Carnforth)
Strathspey Railway
Swanage Railway
Swindon GWR Museum
Swindon & Crickdale Railway
Talyllyn Railway
Tanfield Railway
Teifi Valley Railway
Vale of Rheidol Railway
Wells Harbour Railway
Wells & Walsingham Railway
Welsh Highland Railway
Welshpool & Llanfair Railway
West Somerset Railway
Winchcombe Railway Museum
Paddlesteamer Waverley (sailing details)

FOREWORD

I was particularly pleased to be asked to write this Foreword, for two reasons at least. First, as deputy head of the National Railway Museum, it allows me to praise our friends in the preservation field who are complementing what we are doing in York. I made a study / lecture visit to a number of American Railway Museums earlier this year. In Sacremento I was talking in the display area to the Museum Director, Walter Gray, when a visitor recognising him said "It's a pity the locos in here are not working!" "Oh but they are ", said Walter,"as museum exhibits".

That seemed a very good answer to those who talk of museum exhibits as dead items, stuffed and mounted. We are illustrating in our displays at York, the extraordinary story of the technological and social revolution brought about by the railways, a revolution which really did 'change the world'. Part of that story is the story of the steam engine and the passenger train, but it is much more too - and our rich collections at York reflect that diversity. In April 1992 we re-open the re-roofed Great Hall of the museum and retain the award-winning Great Railway Show, thus doubling our public display space. We shall continue to give working demonstrations and work from time to time on the mainline, but most of our exhibits are 'working' by being on display telling the railway story. And, if over 500,000 people per year come to see them, they are attracting an enviably large public.

What we cannot do at the museum - and this is where I believe we complement the preserved railways, and they us - is to give the actual experience of travelling on a train. Wilson's Timetable lists a wonderful cornucopia of railways both large and small, which do convey that experience and give enormous pleasure to visitors and volunteers alike.

My second reason for accepting David Wilson's invitation to write this Foreword is an exercise in nostalgia. Visits to preserved lines - and my own work at York - nourish that nostalgia. As a child I spent many hours beside the Cambridge cattle-market at the south end of Cambridge Station, watching a busy steam railway scene that has gone forever - not just the steam but quite a lot of the railway too! When I was older I discovered that BR would actually employ me in my school and university holidays. I swept Cambridge Station platform at 02.00am on the night shift, working as an up-end lampman-porter, down-end messenger and, out at Longstanton, as a cut-flower clerk and general station dogsbody. I loved every minute of it and Wilson's Timetable revives those memories.

I welcome the 1992 edition of the Timetable and hope to visit many of the preserved railways during the year - and I hope that you, the reader, will do so too. I also hope you will visit the new National Railway Museum on its enlarged site and enjoy the railway story as much as I have enjoyed the railway experience by riding on a preserved line. Happy memories!

ROB SHORLAND-BALL
Deputy Head, National Railway Museum, York

THE EDITOR'S PAGE

In this, the fourth edition of WILSON'S, I have attempted to be less tongue in cheek in the Wilson's Views, though doubtless there are the odd little passages which may cause a moment of merriment. Hopefully these comments will give you some idea of what one might expect when visiting any of the sites listed. However, it must be remembered that they are only thumb-nail sketches and there is much more to the lines, centres and museums than is covered by my views.

Though this is the fourth edition, it is the first to be published by Argus Books. In my view, as the editor, this is a positive step. The page layout and overall design has greatly improved - though I have to say I regret the loss of the original cover design with its recognisable and distinctive lady. However, this is a small price to pay for what are, I think, improvements in all other respects.

As with previous editions, the TIMETABLE is made possible by the support of advertising revenue. Therefore I would ask you to mention WILSON'S when responding to advertisements or when contacting or visiting the railways listed herein.

ACKNOWLEDGEMENTS
I would like to thank the publicity officers of all the entries for taking the time to send me their details. I would also like to thank Rob Shorland-Ball for his Foreword which echoes the editor's own comments and the men and women of the railways, without whom we wouldn't have a preserved steam railway.

STOCK LISTINGS
The locomotives listed are only those which might operate service trains, or be in operation at special events etc. Before travelling to see a particular locomotive in action please check with the site, as locomotive availability can change rapidly.

Alderney Railway Society

When

| Braye Road | Dep | 14.00 | 15.00 | 16.00 |
| Mannez | Dep | 14.40 | 15.40 | 16.40 |

Weekends, Bank Holidays, Easter Saturday to the end of September.
Note: The 16.00 & 16.40 do not run between Easter and Whitsun.

What

| Easter Egg Special | Easter Sunday |
| Santa Trains | December 21st |

Where

LOCATION
Alderney Railway Society, P.O.Box 75, Alderney, C.I. Telephone (0481) 823534 (Operations Manager).
ACCESS
By Air: Aurigny Air Services from Southampton, Bournemouth, Guernsey and Jersey. Air Sarnia from Southampton, Bournemouth and Guernsey.
By Sea: Torbay Seaways from Torquay.
By Rail: Nearest B.R. is Southampton Parkway for Southampton Airport.
FACILITIES
Shop, Car Park, Disabled Facilities, Refreshments (Sundays only at Mannez).
LOCOS
Bagnall 0-4-0ST No.3 J.T.Daly, Vulcan 0-4-0DM D100 Elizabeth.

Wilson's View

Channel Island steam on the Isle of Alderney is courtesy of the harbour. The original line was constructed to take stone from the quarry to the breakwaters of the harbour, as long ago as 1847. Motive power is provided by Bagnall and coaches by the Tube, making this the `Cosmopolitan Line', if not the `Rock Island Line'.

Alford Valley Railway

When

Alford Dep 11.00 11.30 12.00 12.30 13.00 13.30 14.00 14.30 15.00 15.30 16.00 16.30

Haughton Park to Murray Park trains connect with the service from Alford to Haughton Park. The Alford to Haughton services are steam hauled by a Fowler 0-4-2T and the Haughton Park to Murray Park services are either diesel/steam outline or diesel hauled.

Services operate
Saturday and Sunday in April, May and September. Daily in June July and August.

These details are 1991 listings, no 1992 details received. Intending travellers should check before visiting.

Where
LOCATION
Alford Valley Railway, Alford, Murray Park, Grampian. Telephone (09755) 62326.
ACCESS
By Bus: Services 215 or 220 from Aberdeen.
By Road: Alford is on the A944 from Aberdeen.
By Rail: Aberdeen.
FACILITIES
Shop, Museum, Car & Coach Parking, Provision for Disabled, Nature Trail, Picnic Sites.

Wilson's View
The line in the Highlands with a sweet as sugar Hunslet - a two foot gauge engine of 1912 vintage named Saccharine. The Hunslet operates on the Alford to Haughton Park section; a diesel hauls the service from there to Murray Park. The station at Alford, formerly the property of the Great North of Scotland Railway, is now the home of a museum of transport and a display of GNSR standard gauge items.

Amberley Chalk Pits Museum

NARROW GAUGE BROAD GAUGE STANDARD GAUGE

When
10.00 to 18.00, last admission 17.00.
Services operate from April 1st to November 1st, Wednesday to Sunday.
Daily June 24th to September 13th.

What
Special events throughout the year, details from the office.

Where
LOCATION
Amberley Chalk Pits Museum, Houghton Bridge, Amberley, Arundel, West Sussex BN18 9LT.
Telephone (0798) 831370.
ACCESS
By Road: On B2139 which runs between A29 and A283.
By Rail: Amberley B.R. adjacent.
By Boat: By launch from Arundel or Littlehampton. Phone (0903) 883920.
FACILITIES
Shop, Buffet, Workshops, Amateur Radio Station and Vintage Wireless Exhibition, Nature Trail,
Vintage Buses, Craftsmen demonstrating boatbuilding, Printing, Pottery, Smithying, Steam
traction engines and Road Rollers, Facilities for Disabled.
FARES
Adults 3.90, Senior Citizens 3.00, Children 1.80, Family (2 + 3) 10.50.
LOCOS
Decauville 0-4-0WT Barbouillier, Bagnall 2-4-0T Polar Bear, Bagnall 0-4-0ST Peter, Baldwin
4-6-0T Lion, Fletcher Jennings 0-4-0T Townsend Hook, Pecket 0-6-0T Scaldwell, Motor Rail
No. 11001 Ibstock, Diesels Hudson Hunslet No 3097, Wingrove & Rogers No 4998.

Wilson's View
`Trains n' Boats and Buses'?; even an amateur radio station is to be found in this
rehabilitated chalk mining operation. There are traction engines as well as railway, nature
trails and demonstrations of the art of boat building, smithying and pottering - indeed, such
is the variety of things to see and do, that the museum recommends allowing a minimum of
three hours to get the most out of any visit.

Avon Valley Railway

STANDARD GAUGE

When
Bitton Station is open every weekend for viewing of locomotives and rolling stock. Steam trains
operate from 11.00 to 17.00 on the following dates: April 17-20th, May 3,4,24 and 25th, June
7th, July 5,12,19 and 26th, August 2,9,16,23,30 and 31st, September 6 and 27th, October 4th,
November 28-29th, December 5,6,12,13,19,20,23,24,26 and 27th and January 1st 1993.

What
Friends of Thomas	June 7th
Heavy Horse Days	July 5th, August 2nd, October 4th
Teddy Bears Picnic	July 19th
Railways on Canvas	August 30-31st
Steaming for Barnado's	September 27th
Santa Trains	November 28-29th, December 5,6,12,13,19,20,23 and 24th
Mince Pie Trains	December 26-27th, January 1st 1993

Where

LOCATION
Bitton Station, Willsbridge, Bristol, BS15 6ED. Telephone (0272) 327296.
ACCESS
By Bus: Bristol Omnibus Services 332 & 58.
By Road: Bitton Station is on the A431 from Bristol to Bath.
By Rail: Bristol Temple Meads.
FACILITIES
Shop/Buffet, Museum, Car & Coach Parking.
LOCOS
Manning Wardle 0-6-OT Littleton.
FARES
Adults 2.20 Children/OAP 1.30 Family (2 + 2) 5.70.

Wilson's View

This year, the railway are operating over their new section which was opened at Easter last year. An interesting addition to the visitor attractions at the Bitton terminus is a working heavy horse harnessed to a restored LMS horse dray. The railway will also be home, for a season, to the rebuilt M7 30053 and the Port Line Project will be working here to restore the Class 4 Standard Tank 80104.

Ayrshire Railway Preservation Group

STANDARD GAUGE

When

11.00 to 16.00. Open days with steam hauled brake van rides: Sunday May 31st, Saturday & Sunday June 27-28th, July 5,12,19,25 and 26th, August 9, 29 and 30th, September 27th.
NB: On Sundays June 28th, July 26th and August 30th the fireless loco will be in steam. The site is open for static display on Saturdays from June to September 30th.

Where

LOCATION
Minnivey Colliery, Nr.Dalmellington, Strathclyde. Telephone (0292) 313579 Postal Address: Mr. G. Thomson, 8 Burnside Place, Troon, Ayrshire KA10 6LZ.
Doon Valley Heritage Office Phone: (0292) 531144. Daytimes only - for special event details.
ACCESS
By Bus: Western Scottish Services from Ayr to Castle Douglas.
By Road: On A713 Ayr/Castle Douglas road, signposted.
By Rail: Ayr.
FACILITIES
Shop, Buffet, Car & Coach Parking, Some Provision for Disables, 2'6" gauge line under construction.

Wilson's View

Based on a former colliery line, the Group now offer steam railway services in conjunction with a museum of mining based in the former Minnivey Colliery. The group acquired a greenfield site at the demolished Minnivey Colliery in 1980, and all the trackwork and the loco shed have been built by the volunteers. The group have also taken over the former colliery workshops, which are now a museum and shop. The eventual aim of the ARPG is to run a service between Minnivey and Dunaskin where an industrial heritage centre is being created - no silly jokes about Dunaskin, Dunsteamin, Dunroamin, Dunrobin!

Bala Lake Railway

When

		A	B	A	B	A	B	A	B	A
Llanuwchllyn	Dep	11.00	11.15	12.30	12.50	14.00	14.25	15.30	16.00	17.00
Bala	Arr	11.25	11.40	12.55	13.15	14.25	14.50	15.55	16.25	17.25
Bala	Dep	11.35	11.50	13.05	13.25	14.35	15.00	16.05	16.35	17.30
Llanuwchllyn	Arr	12.00	12.15	13.30	13.50	15.00	15.25	16.30	17.00	17.55

A: Operates May 23-31st, July 18th to September 6th.
B: Operates daily April 11-26th (except Fridays April 27th to May 21st and June 1-25th). Daily from June 27th to July 17th (except Fridays September 7th to October 4th). Extra trains may run on Bank Holidays and during peak periods.

Where

LOCATION
Llanuwchllyn Station, Llanuwchllyn, Bala, Gwynedd. Telephone (06784) 666.
ACCESS
By Bus: From Wrexham or Barmouth service D94 or D93.
By Road: Off the A494 Bala/Dolgellau Road from the North take signs for Bala , from the South take signs for Llanuwchllyn.
By Rail: Barmouth or Ruabon.
FACILITIES
Shop, Buffet, Provision for Disabled Access, Museum, Car Parking, Picnic Site (Llangower Station).
LOCOS
Hunslet 0-4-0 ST's Holy War & Maid Marion.
FARES
Adults 4.00 return, Children 2.00, Family fares 2 adults + 1 child 9.00, 2 adults + 2 children 10.00.

Wilson's View

The only railway in the country to be able to boast not only Maid Marion but a Holy War as well! However, Bala Lake's Maid Marion is not the buxom wench in Lincoln Green and the Holy War is actually an 0-4-0ST built by Hunslet's of Leeds, as is Maid Marion. Perhaps instead of a fat controller on Thomas Days, they should have the Sheriff of Nottingham, or possibly Friar Tuck.

Beamish Open Air Museum

STANDARD GAUGE

When
April to October, 10.00 to 18.00 daily.
November to March, 10.00 to 17.00 Tuesday to Sunday.
Last admission 16.00.

What
Events throughout the year, contact the museum for details.

Where
LOCATION
Beamish Open Air Museum, Beamish, Co Durham DH9 0RG. Telephone (0207) 231811.
ACCESS
By Bus: From Newcastle, Sunderland and Durham. On summer Sundays and Bank Holidays a special service runs from Durham & Newcastle No X75 from Eldon Square, Newcastle and No X79 from Durham railway station. Service 720 runs from Durham plus services from Newcastle and Sunderland to Beamish Crossing, close to the museum.
By Road: Off A693 Stanley to Chester-le-Street, signposted from A1M.
By Rail: Durham or Newcastle.
FACILITIES
Shop, Buffet, Pub, Tramway system, Farm, Mining Exhibitions, Car & Coach Parking.
LOCOS
0-4-0ST No14, 0-4-0 No1 Locomotion (replica). Others under restoration including a Class J21 65033.
TRAMS
Gateshead No10 Blackpool, No31, Sheffield No264.
FARES
Summer season: Adults 5.00 Children/OAP 4.00. Winter: Adults 3.00 Children/OAP 2.50.
(1991 rates only).

Wilson's View
A new entry for 1992 but not a new museum. Beamish has been around for some twenty years now and offers a whole spectrum of life from years gone by. There is a colliery village, a station - ex-Rowley on the Consett to Burnhill route of the North Eastern Railway. To complement the station there is a signal box, coal sidings and a variety of station goods vehicles. Steam is used during the summer season on demonstration freight workings, though there are some passenger trains too. The railway is only a part of the attractions of Beamish. There are trams, a couple of farms, traction engines, a mine and a drift pit, and if you look closely you may even spot Tom and Cobbley an' all!

Opposite: Derek Foster's Standard 4 Mogul 76079 rolls into Ramsbottom station with the 15.00 hrs ex Bury.

Bluebell Railway

STANDARD GAUGE

When

Table A

Sheffield Park	Dep	10.20	11.00	11.40	12.20	13.00	13.40	14.20	15.00	15.40	16.20	17.00 17.40
Horsted Keynes	Arr	10.35	11.15	11.55	12.35	13.15	13.55	14.35	15.15	15.55	16.35	17.15 17.55
Horsted Keynes	Dep	10.40	11.20	12.00	12.40	13.20	14.00	14.40	15.20	16.00	16.40	17.20
New Coombe B.	Arr	10.50	11.30	12.10	12.50	13.30	14.10	14.50	15.30	16.10	16.50	17.30

New Coombe B.	Dep		10.58	11.38	12.18	12.58	13.38	14.18	14.58	15.38	16.18	16.58 17.38
Horsted Keynes	Arr		11.06	11.46	12.26	13.06	13.46	14.26	15.06	15.46	16.26	17.06 17.46

Horsted Keynes	Dep	10.37	11.18	11.58	12.38	13.18	13.58	14.38	15.18	15.58	16.38	17.18 17.58
Sheffield Park	Arr	10.50	11.31	12.11	12.51	13.31	14.11	14.51	15.31	16.11	16.51	17.31 18.11

Table B

		A	A	A	A	A	A
Sheffield Park	Dep	11.00	12.10	13.20	14.30	15.40	16.50
Horsted Keynes	Arr	11.15	12.25	13.35	14.45	15.55	17.05
Horsted Keynes	Dep	11.17	12.27	13.37	14.47	15.57	17.07
New Coombe Bridge	Arr	11.27	12.37	13.47	14.57	16.07	17.17
New Coombe Bridge	Dep	11.37	12.47	13.57	15.07	16.17	17.27
Horsted Keynes	Arr	11.45	12.55	14.05	15.15	16.25	17.35
Horsted Keynes	Dep	11.47	12.57	14.07	15.17	16.27	17.37
Sheffield Park	Arr	12.00	13.10	14.20	15.30	16.40	17.50

Table C

Sheffield Park	Dep	11.15	12.45	14.15	15.45
Horsted Keynes	Arr	11.30	13.00	14.30	16.00
Horsted Keynes	Dep	11.32	13.02	14.32	16.02
New Coombe Bridge	Arr	11.42	13.12	14.42	16.12
New Coombe Bridge	Dep	11.52	13.22	14.52	16.22
Horsted Keynes	Arr	12.00	13.30	15.00	16.30
Horsted Keynes	Dep	12.02	13.32	15.02	16.32
Sheffield Park	Arr	12.15	13.45	15.15	16.45

Notes: (A) shuttle connection with these services until the re-opening of the Horsted Keynes to New Coombe Bridge section.

Service Operates:
Table A
April 17th to 20th, May 3rd/4th/10/17/24/25/31st, July 19/26th, August 2/9/16/23/30/31st, September 6/13th.
Table B
March 8/15/22/29th, April 4/5/11/12/25/26th, May 9/16/23/30th, June 6/7/13/14/20/21/27/28th, July 4/5/11th to 18th/20th to 25th/27th to August 1st, 3rd to 8th/10th to 15th/17th to 22nd/24th to 29th, September 1st to 5th/12/19/20/26/27th, October 4/11/18/25th.
Table C
January 5/12/19/26th, February 2/9/16/23rd, March 1/7/14/21/28th, April 21st to 24th, May 6/13/20/27th, June 1st to 5th/8th to 12th/15th to 19th/22nd to 26th, June 29th to July 3rd/6th to 10th, September 7th to 11th/14th to 18th/21st to 25th/28th to 30th, October 3/10/17/19th to 24th/26th to 31st, November 1/7/8/14/15/21/22/28th.

What

Re-opening of Horsted Keynes to New Coombe Bridge dates to be announced in the press.
Santa Trains run November 29th, December 5/6/12/13/18th to 24th.
Mince Pie Trains run December 26/27th.
Booking is essential for Santa trains phone for a leaflet (available September).
Shuttle service will continue until the line to New Coombe Bridge re-opens. Once the line re-opens the timings are those above. The shuttle does not run on table C dates, but if the re-opening occurs during these dates the service to New Coombe Bridge will run.

Where

LOCATION:
Sheffield Park Station, Nr Uckfield, Sussex. Telephone (082) 5722370 or 3777 for Office.
ACCESS:
By Bus: From Haywards Heath Southdown Service 769. B.R. run a road rail link during the Summer and at weekends in Winter.
By Road: Sheffield Park Station is on the A275 just a mile or two from its junction with the A272.
By Rail: Haywards Heath.
FACILITIES: Buffet (Sheffield Park & Horsted Keynes), Restaurant Sheffield Park, Shops, Museum, Provision for Disabled, Car Parking, Picnic Site.
LOCOS: Ex-B.R. 9F 92240, Ex-S.R. 30928 Stowe, Ex-S.R. 4-6-2 35027 Port Line, Ex-S.R. 0-6-0 541, Ex S.R. 2-6-0 1618, Ex-LSWR 4-4-2T 488, Ex-GWR 4-4-0 3217 Earl of Berkeley, Ex-LBSCR 0-6-0T Stepney, Ex-NLR 0-6-0T 2650.
FARES: Adults 4.00, Children (3-13) 2.00, Shuttle Fares 1.00&50pence, Supplement for 1st Class. Platform Tickets at Sheffield Park 1.00 & 50pence, Horsted Keynes 50 pence & 25 pence. Special rates for parties. These are the 1991 rates, those for 1992 have not been advised.

Wilson's View

Now in its thirty-second year, the Bluebell is one of preservation's `elder statesmen', yet it is still in the process of expanding its track mileage. During the 1991 season the line added yet another major TV spectacular to its long list of starring roles, when it was the setting for Channel 4's Steam Sunday, the curtain raiser to the Going Loco series.
Bluebell Railway is also the home of the Clive Groome Firing & Driving Courses, and to a most comprehensive selection of ex-Southern Railways rolling stock and locos.

Bodmin & Wenford Railway

STANDARD GAUGE

When

10.00 to 17.00 Easter to end of October.
Service operates: April 17-22, 26 and 29th. May 3, 4, 6, 10, 13, 17, 20 and 24th, then daily until July 11th (except Saturdays). Daily from July 12th to September 30th. Sundays October 4, 11, 18 and 25th. December 5, 6, 12, 13, 19, 20-24th and 27th.
During 1992 a new station will be opened at Fletchersbridge, serving Cardinham Woods and Bodmin Park Farm.
Special evening services run July 22, 29th. August 5, 12, 19 and 26th & September 2nd. These services are steam hauled and depart at 19.30.

What

Traction Engine Display	April 19-20th
Bodmin Branch Birthday	May 31st
Friends of Thomas Weekend	September 5-6th
Autumn Steam Gala	September 13th
Santa Trains	December 7, 8, 14, 15, 21 and 22nd

Where

LOCATION
Bodmin General Station, Bodmin, Cornwall PL31 1AQ. Telephone (0208) 73666/74878.
ACCESS
By Bus: Western National Services.
By Road: Just South of Bodmin town centre on B3268 Lostwithiel Road.
By Rail: Bodmin Parkway.
By Bike: Hire in Wadebridge then via Camel Trail.
FACILITIES
Shop, Buffet, Heritage Centre.
FARES
To be announced.
LOCOS
Austerity 0-6-0ST Swiftsure, 0-6-0ST Glendower, 0-6-0ST Ugly, Guest Loco.

Wilson's View

Bodmin, the sort of place one expects to bump into Sherlock Holmes hotly pursued by a gnashing Pit Bull Terrier, or at least en-route to Baskerville Hall. In reality, of course, on arrival at Bodmin one will be greeted by the whistle of a steam engine rather than the howl of some devilish hound, the only screeching that of flanges on curves, and the only barking will be the exhaust beat of the engine as it toils up the gradients on this four mile run through woods, dales and Cornish glades.

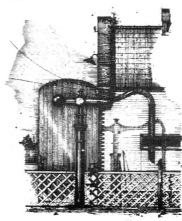

Bo'ness & Kinneil Railway

STANDARD GAUGE

The Forth Valley Line

When

		A	B				D
Bo'ness	Dep	11.05	12.10	13.15	14.20	15.25	16.30
Kinneil	Dep	11.13	12.18	13.23	14.28	15.33	16.38
Birkhill	Arr	11.22	12.27	13.32	14.37	15.42	16.47

		A	B				D
Birkhill	Dep	11.32	12.37	13.42	14.47	15.52	17.00
Kinneil	Dep	11.41	12.46	13.51	14.56	16.01	17.09
Bo'ness	Arr	11.49	12.54	13.59	15.04	16.09	17.17

(A) only runs July & August & special event days. (B) Not Saturdays in April & May. (D) Diesel. Trains pick up and set down at Kinneil on a signal to the guard or driver.

Service operates

Saturdays & Sundays April 11th to October 18th & November 28th to December 20th. Bank Holiday Mondays April 20th, May 4th/25th & August 31st. School weeks May 25th to 29th & June 1st to 5th. High Season daily July 18th to August 31st.

What

Easter Egg Specials	April 18th to 20th.
Friends of Thomas Events	May 16th/17th & August 15th/16th.
Victorian Street Fair	Sunday May 24th.
Schools Weeks	May 25th-29th & June 1st-5th.
Teddy Bears Picnic	Sunday June 14th.
Veteran Car Rally	Sunday June 21st.
Historic Commercial Rally	September 20th.
Diesel Enthusiasts Weekend	September 26th/27th.
Santa Season	Sats & Suns November 30th to December 22nd.

Where

LOCATION: Bo'ness Station, Union Street, Bo'ness, West Lothian, EH51 OAD Telephone (0506) 822298.

ACCESS: By Bus: From Glasgow, Bluebird Express Service X17 Midland Bluebird Service 37/X37 (Via Falkirk) From Edinburgh, Bluebird Express Service X19/X20. Midland Bluebird Services 45/48.

By Rail: Falkirk (Grahamstown), Linlithgow.

By Road: Motorway M9 to Jct 3 then A904 or Jct 5 then A905/A904.

FACILITIES: Car Parking (free), Refreshment Room, Shop, Loco Shed, Picnic Area, Visitor Trail & Guided Tours on request. Go underground at Birkhill Fireclay Mine.

FARES: Adults 3.00 Child/OAP 2.00 Family 7.50 (2 adults & 2 children) Party Rates on application. Fares may vary at some special events, Thomas days and Santa specials.

LOCOS: Ex-LMS 4-6-0 44871 Sovereign, Ex-N.B 0-6-0 Maude, Barclay 0-4OST No. 3 Clydesmill, Ex-NCB Austerity No 19 Diesels D5351, D5347, D7585, D8020 etc.

Wilson's View

Go Forth, and they did, multiplying the length of their line and bringing back Maude, that's General not Garden Maude, and, like the line, Maude is of North British descent. Enough of this ribald nonsense, the BKR has a line and record to be proud of - stations, rolling stock and locos, all with a uniquely Scottish flavour and all taking place almost in sight of one of the most famous railway bridges in the World - The Forth Bridge. At Birkhill there's a chance to visit a clay mine and go underground, and at Bo'ness there are some excellently restored goods wagons and goods handling facilities.

Bowes Railway.

STANDARD GAUGE

When
Service operates   12.00 to 17.00
April 19th/20th, May 3/4/17/24/25th June 7/21st . July 5/19th.
August 2/16/30/31st . September 6/20th. December 6/12/13/20th.
Open for static display on Saturdays.

What
Santa Trains December 6/12/13/20th.

Where
LOCATION: Bowes Railway, Springwell Village, Nr Gateshead , Tyne & Wear ,
Telephone office hours: (091) 4161847.
ACCESS: By Bus: Gateshead Metro Services 187/8/9, X4,X5,X94.
By Road: On B1288 off A1(M).
By Rail: Newcastle-Upon-Tyne.
FACILITIES: Shop, Buffet, Guided Tours, Exhibition of Wagons, 2 Rope Hauled Incline,
Stationary Winding Engines, Car & Coach Parking (Springwell).
LOCOS: 2 Barclay 0-4-OST,RSH 0-6-OST, Hunslet 0-6-0 Diesel, Hibberd & Barclay Diesel.
FARES: Adults 2.00, Children/OAP 1.00, Family (2 + 2) 5.00, Group rates on application
(inc train rides). Prices may vary on special theme days i.e. Thomas Days etc.

Wilson's View
**A real piece of history and the only operational rope-worked incline in existence. The Bowes
Railway has a history that goes back to the dawn of railways and the small exhibits museum,
the brain child of Bill Craddock, a great champion of the Bowes Railway, is a must for any
visitor. The museum shows the intimate links between coal, the Tyne and the ancestry of
the railway age. The Bowes Railway also boasts a representative of every type of wagon used
by the Bowes Railway, which was formerly the Pontop and Jarrow. The antiquities are
complemented by a modern shop and cafe with - yes, you've guessed, an excellent line in
buns and coffee.**

Brecon Mountain Railway.

NARROW GAUGE

When

		A						X
Pant	Dep	11.00	12.00	13.00	14.00	15.00	16.00	17.00
Taf fechan	Dep	11.35	12.35	13.35	14.35	15.35	16.35	17.35

Round trip time 50 minutes including a 20 minute stopover at Taf fechan reservoir.

Notes:
A: Runs April 17th to 26th, May 1st to 4th & 23rd to 31st, Sundays excepted, May 5th to 22nd,
Daily May 23rd to September 6th Sunday, Monday & Fridays excepted, September 8th to
October 3rd.
X: Runs April 17th to 26th, May 2nd to 4th & 23rd to 31st, Sundays only June 7th to 28th, daily
4th July to September 6th.

Service Operates
April 5th to 17th Sundays only. Daily April 17th to 26th & May 1st to September 6th. Mondays
& Fridays excepted from September 8th to October 3rd, Sundays only October 3rd to 18th and
daily October 25th to 31st.
N.B. No road access to Pontsticill, passengers should join at Pant Station.

Where

LOCATION: Pant Station, Dowlais, Merthyr Tydfil, Mid-Glamorgan. Telephone (0685) 384854.
ACCESS: By Bus: From Merthyr Tydfil to Pant cemetery.
By Rail: Merthyr Tydfil from Cardiff.
By Road: Off the A465 about 3 miles north of Merthyr Tydfil.
FACILITIES: Shop, Buffet(Pontsticill), Car & Coach Parking(Pant), Restaurant(Pant), Some Provision for Disabled, Picnic Site.
LOCOS: 0-6-2WTT Graf Schwerin-Lowitz and later in year 4-6-2 Baldwin.
FARES: Adults 3.60 one child free with each adult others 1.80. Fares include admission to the workshops.

Wilson's View

An excellent terminus building and workshops, a very scenic route and a caboose-style coach to enjoy it from. A trackbed being extended deeper into the Brecons by the shores of a lake, a 1930s Baldwin Pacific being rebuilt to run on the extension, all go to give the impression of a well-run, well-ordered railway.

Bressingham Steam Museum & Gardens

When

STANDARD GAUGE
NARROW GAUGE
MINIMUM GAUGE

10.00 to 17.30
The Museum is open daily from April 1st to October 31st.
Steam days are every Sunday, Thursday and Bank Holiday from April 1st to October 31st, also Wednesdays in July and August.

What

Special opening and events November 29th to December 20th.

Where

LOCATION
Bressingham Hall, Diss, Norfolk. Telephone (037988)382/6.
ACCESS
By Road: 2.5 miles west of Diss on A1066
By Rail: Diss
FACILITIES
Shop, Buffet, Provision for Disabled, Car & Coach Parking, Large Gardens, Victorian Steam Horses (Gallopers), Footplate Rides, Picnic Areas.
FARES
Adults 2.50, children 1.50 (train rides not included).
LOCOS
Ex-Norwegian Railways 2-6-0 King Haakon 7, Ex-Waveney Valley 15" gauge Krupps 4-6-2'S Mannertreu, Rosenkavalier, 2" gauge 0-6-0WT Bronllwyd 0-4-0ST George Sholto, 9.5" gauge 4-4-2 Princess, Replica 15" gauge Flying Scotsman used as relief loco on 15" gauge circuit.

Wilson's View

Lots of gauges, lines and locos set in gardens that have featured on the TV. Traction engines and railway ones, steam driven gallopers, quite a collection of things that puff, chuff, wheeze and clank are all to be savoured at Bressingham. What is perhaps even more startling is that this is a private collection, which includes such notables as a Britannia No.70013 Oliver Cromwell, an ex-London Tilbury and Southend Railway 4-4-2 Thundersley, a Royal Scot, a Stanier 2-6-4T No.2500, a Duchess, a Terrier and a variety of other BR industrial and foreign locos. It must be said that some of the locos are part of the National Collection, i.e. 70013, Thundersley, and a GER 0-6-0 designed by Holden and built in 1905, BR No. 65567.

Bristol Harbour Railway

STANDARD GAUGE

When

12.00 to 18.00
Trains run at 15 minute intervals between Maritime Heritage Centre (S.S. Great Britain).
Service Operates
March 28th/29th.   April 11/12/18/19/20th. May 2-4th/9/10/23-25th.
June if no power boat racing 6/7/20/21st, if there is power boat racing 27/28th
July if no power boat racing 4/5th, if there is 11/12/18th
August 1/2/29-31st. September 12/13/26/27th. October 10/11/24/25/31st. November 1st.

Where

LOCATION
Bristol Industrial Museum, Princes Wharf, Bristol BS1 4RN. Telephone (0272) 251470.
ACCESS
By Bus: Services from Bristol town centre.
By Road: Bristol is off M5 and docks are in town centre close to Temple Meads Station.
By Rail: Bristol Temple Meads.
FACILITIES
Shop, Car Parking, Mayflower Steam Tug Operates From The Docks, Heritage Centre, No
Access To Locos On Non Steam Days.
LOCOS
Avonside 0-6-0ST Portway, Peckett 0-6-0ST Henbury.

Wilson's View

Using Bristol-built locos, one an Avonside, the other a Peckett, the volunteers of the Bristol
Harbour Railway run a service between the Industrial Museum and the Maritime Heritage
Centre based in the SS Great Britain. The line itself is part of a hundred-year-old system
built to link the docks with the mainline railways. The volunteers have also restored to
service a number of the former Harbour Co's own wagons.

Buckinghamshire Railway Centre

Quainton Railway Society.

When

Steam Days   11.00 to 18.00 (Last Admission 17.00)
Non-Steam Days   11.00 to 16.00
Steam Days: Every Sunday and Bank Holiday from Easter Sunday to the end of October.
Wednesday from June to September.
Non-Steam Days: Good Friday, Easter Saturday, and every Saturday to end of October.

Where

LOCATION
The Railway Station, Quainton Nr. Aylesbury, Bucks HP22 4BY. Telephone (029675)450.
ACCESS
By Bus: Red Rover from Aylesbury.
By Road: Off A41 at Waddesdon 5 miles NW of Aylesbury.
By Rail: Aylesbury (Charter shuttle some Bank Holidays).
FACILITIES
Shop, Buffet, Car Parking, Some Provision For Disabled, Small Exhibits Museum, Victorian Tea Specials(booking essential), Served In LNWR Dining Car, Children's Birthday Parties (booking essential).
LOCOS
Metropolitan No. 1 Ex-GWR 0-6-0PT L99 Coventry, Sentinels, visiting locos.
FARES
Steam days, Adults 3.00, children and senior citizens 2.00, Family 2 Adults and up to 5 children 8.00. Non-Steam days Adults 1.50, children and senior citizens 1.00. (1991 prices, 1992 not advised)

Wilson's View

Victorian afternoon tea in a former Royal Saloon, a truly minute 0-4-0T Peckett, Metropolitan No.1, a Hawksworth Pannier and, hidden away in a quiet corner, a couple of Stanier Prairies - mouthwatering. There's a steam rail car from, Egypt, built by Sentinel/Scammell - an extraordinary machine and, from a monster of a rail car to a diminutive oddity, the 1874 Vintage Beattie Well Tank. This tiny 2-4-0WT remained in active duty until 1962, working the Wenford branch in Cornwall, a section of which may well become part of the Bodmin and Wenford Railway's running line. All this, and more, is to be found at BRC.

Bure Valley Railway

When

Table A

Aylsham	Dep	10.10	11.20	12.30	14.00	15.10	16.20	17.30
Brampton	Dep	10.23	11.33	12.43	14.13	15.23	16.33	17.43
Buxton	Dep	10.29	11.39	12.49	14.19	15.29	16.39	17.49
Coltishall	Dep	10.44	11.54	13.04	14.34	15.44	16.54	18.04
Wroxham	Arr	10.56	12.06	13.16	14.46	15.56	17.06	18.16

								X
Wroxham	Dep	10.10	11.20	12.30	14.00	15.10	16.20	17.30
Coltishall	Dep	10.25	11.35	12.45	14.15	15.25	16.35	17.45
Buxton	Dep	10.39	11.49	12.59	14.29	15.39	16.49	17.59
Brampton	Dep	10.44	11.54	13.04	14.34	15.44	16.54	18.04
Aylsham	Arr	10.56	12.06	13.16	14.46	15.56	17.06	18.16

Table B

Aylsham	Dep	10.15	12.15	14.15	16.15
Brampton	Dep	10.28	12.28	14.28	16.28
Buxton	Dep	10.34	12.34	14.34	16.34
Coltishall	Dep	10.49	12.49	14.49	16.49
Wroxham	Arr	11.01	13.01	15.01	17.01

Wroxham	Dep	11.15	13.15	15.15	17.15
Coltishall	Dep	11.30	13.30	15.30	17.30
Buxton	Dep	11.44	13.44	15.44	17.44
Brampton	Dep	11.49	13.49	15.49	17.49
Aylsham	Arr	12.01	14.01	16.01	18.01

Table C

Aylsham	Dep	11.00	13.15	15.15
Brampton	Dep	11.13	13.28	15.28
Buxton	Dep	11.19	13.34	15.34
Coltishall	Dep	11.34	13.49	15.49
Wroxham	Arr	11.46	14.01	16.01

Wroxham	Dep	12.00	14.15	16.15
Coltishall	Dep	12.15	14.30	16.30
Buxton	Dep	12.29	14.44	16.44
Brampton	Dep	12.34	14.49	16.49
Aylsham	Arr	12.46	15.01	17.01

Notes. X runs only from July 19th to September 3rd & on weekend October 3/4th.
Trains connect with B.R Services at Wroxham.

Services Operate
Table A
April 17th-20th, May 24th-29th, July except 3/4/10/11/18th, daily August 1st to September 13th & October 3/4th.
Table B
April 21st-26th, May 2nd-4th/10th/17th/30th-31st, June 1st-4th/7th-11th/14th-18th/21st-25th/28th-30th, July 3/4/10/11/17/18th, September 14th-30th, October 18th-24th.
Table C
May 5th-7th/11th-14th/18th-21st, October 5th-7th/10th-14th/17th.

What

Gala Weekend	October 3/4th
Boat Train	The 10.15 ex-Aylsham will connect with a boat tour of the Broads
Santa Trains	December 5/6/12/13/19-22nd

Where

LOCATION
Bure Valley Railway, Norwich Road, Aylsham, Norfolk. Telephone 0263-733858.
ACCESS
By Bus: Eastern Counties services to Aylsham or Wroxham.
By Car: Aylsham is on the A140 Norwich/Cromer Road, in Norwich Road at the start of Aylsham By-pass.
By Rail: Wroxham (Adjacent).

FACILITIES
Shop, Restaurant(Aylsham), Tourist Information, Car Parking, Trackside Walk, Facilities For Disabled, Bus Link To Blickling Hall.
LOCOS
NO.24, Sidney, and visiting Locos.
FARES
Adults 6.00, O.A.P. 5.00, Children 3.50. Family (2 + 2) 16.50.

Wilson's View

Now 'under new management', Bure Valley Railway has had a chequered start to its life. Brought into being by a leisure company, which subsquently felt the chill wind of recession, the line is now in the hands of the Hart family - perhaps best known for their involvement in the Ffestiniog Railway. There are plans to bring new engines to the line, including the possibility of a re-gauged 2' loco which would become the most powerful 15" gauge loco in the country. There could well be some interesting and historic locos at work over this nine mile route during 1992. Definitely a line to watch out for this year.

Cadeby Light Railway

NARROW GAUGE

When

January 11th. February 8th. March 7th. April 11th. May 9th. June 13th. July 11th. August 8th. September 12th. October 10th. November 7th (Bonfire party) and 14th. December 12th (Santa Special) and 26th (Mince Pie Special). Contact the line for timetable details.

Where

LOCATION
The Old Rectory, Cadeby, Leicestershire.
Telephone (0455) 290462.
ACCESS
By Bus: From Hinckley or Market Bosworth or Leicester.
By Road: On A447 between Hinckley and Coalville.
By Rail: Hinckley.
FACILITIES
Boston Museum.
LOCOS
0-4-0 St Pixie, 0-4-0 WT Orenstein & Koppel.
FARES
Donations.

Wilson's View

Plenty of brass here - the rubbing, not spending variety. The Cadeby Light Railway was the result of the labours of the late Reverend Boston and is today run by his widow with the help of those volunteers who supported the Reverend Boston. In addition to the steam railway, there is the timetabled model railway and, of course, the brass rubbing.

TUNBRIDGE WELLS WEST

Caledonian Railway

When

11.00 to 16.00 Subject to inspection by H.M.R.I. An all-line service (Brechin-Bridge of Dun) will run on Sundays from May 3rd to August 30th. There will also be special events on dates listed below and the sites at Brechin & Bridge of Dun are staffed on most weekends.

What

Easter Special	April 19th
Gala Day	July 19th
Halloween	October 25th
Santa Trains	December 6/13/20th

Where

LOCATION
Caledonian Railway(Brechin) Ltd. The Station, 2 Park Road, Brechin DD9 7AF.
Telephone (0334) 55965 Monday to Friday after 4.30pm.
ACCESS
By Road: Off A94 follow Montrose signs through town centre to Southesk Street or via A935 from Montrose or A933 from Arbroath, second left in Southesk Street signed tourist information and station is directly ahead.
By Rail: Montrose (9 miles).
FACILITIES
Shop, Buffet, Car & Coach Parking, Picnic Area (Bridge of Dun), Charter Train Service.
FARES
Shuttle service adults 1.40, O.A.P./Children 0.70, Full line service adult 3.00
O.A.P./Children 1.50. (1991 prices).
LOCOS
Hunslet Austerity No1 Diana, Bagnall 0-6-OST No.6, Barclay 0-4-OST No.1,
BR Class 20 20056, Class 08 D3059, Class 02 D2866.

Wilson's View

Another of the North of the Border railways and, as its name suggests, it was once a part of the Caledonian system. The line's Eastern terminus at Bridge of Dun is not more than a stone's throw from the famous Kinnaber Junction of `Railway Race to the North' fame, though there'll be no racing on the Caley today. However, there are still steam trains and a super line in Bacon butties.

Chasewater Light Railway

When

No details were received from this site but contact details have been included . Intending visitors should draw their own conclusions and try to contact the line before making any visits.

Where

LOCATION
Chasewater park, Brownhills, West Midlands Telephone (0543) 452623
ACCESS
By Bus: West Midlands Travel 154/6 from Birmingham, or 345/396 from Walsall.
By Road: On Pool Road off southbound carriageway of A5 at Brownhills
By Rail: Birmingham or Monday - Saturday Walsall

Shop, Buffet, Picnic Areas, Lakeside Walk, Extensive Railway Relics, Collection, Car and Coach Parking.
LOCOS
Hawthorn Leslie 0-4-0ST Asbestos, Peckett 0-4-0ST Lion, Sentinel VBT No 57
FARES
Adults 1.00 Children .50p (unlimited rides) (1991 prices, 1992 not advised).

Wilson's View

Once part of the Cannock Chase & Wolverhampton Railway, later the Midland, this line was one of the earliest in preservation. The line runs beside a reservoir built to supply water to the Birmingham canals, though today it's the haunt of many species of water fowl and boating enthusiasts. In addition to the fleet of ex-industrial locos, there are examples of Victorian rolling stock originall in use on the Cannock & Rugely colliery lines. There is also a fine small exhibits display to be found at Chasewater and, for the kids, there is a play area in addition to the lakeside walks and picnic spots.

Chatterley Whitfield Mining Museum

STANDARD GAUGE

When

Daily except Christmas Day 10.00hrs to 17.00hrs
Underground trips 10.00hrs to 16.00hrs

What

Events throughout the year advertised in the local press.

Where

LOCATION
Chatterley Whitfield Mining Museum, Tunstall, Stoke-On-Trent, Staffordshire ST6 8UN.
Telephone (0782) 747000.
ACCESS
By Bus: From Newcastle-Under-Lyme or Hanley (Special buses on Sundays) - contact Potteries Motor Transport for full details.
By Road: Off the A527 Tunstall to Congleton Road, follow Heritage Trail signs.
By Rail: Stoke-On-Trent
FACILITIES
Shop, Buffet, Conference Facilities, Educational Services, Guide Services.
FARES
Adults 3.85, Children/Students/O.A.P. 2.85, Family 11.75.

Wilson's View

This former colliery is now home to a museum of mining and houses part of the NCB's collection of steam locomotives in addition to numerous diesel and electric locos of both standard and narrow gauge, these latter are used to give rides underground, whilst the former give demonstrations of shunting etc. The museum also has displays of working pit machinery and has both pit ponies and dray horses at work. Chatterley Whitfield is a classic example of the working museum and it gives the visitor a real insight into the links between King Coal and the power that he held when steam ran everything.

Chinnor & Princes Risborough Railway Ass

STANDARD GAUGE

When

The Association hope to be able to commence limited operations during this year, anyone wishing to pay a visit to this new railway should contact Mr P Harris on (0296) 433795.

Where

LOCATION
Princes Risborough
ACCESS
For details of access contact above
LOCOS
Sentinel 0-4-0VBTG No6515, Diesels Baguley 0-4-0 Boris, Ex-BR Class 17 D8568.

Wilson's View

One of the newest of preservation schemes, the C&PRRA hope to be able to operate on several weekends during 1992 over a three mile stretch of what was once the Princes Risborough to Watlington branch of the Great Western Railway. During 1991 the railway successfully bid for the redundant semaphore signalling from Princes Risborough, which will in due course be put back in action on the branch.

Cholsey & Wallingford Railway

STANDARD GAUGE

When

Every Sunday Easter to September 20th 11.00 to 17.00.
Steam Trains Operate: Frequently between 13.00 and 16.30, on the first and third Sundays of each month at special events listed below and on all Bank Holidays.

What

Cholsey Centenary	February 29th
Easter Bunny Specials	April 19th/20th (Wallingford)
May Day Celebrations	May 2nd (Cholsey)
Teddy Bears Picnic	July 19th (Wallingford)
Flower Show	August 8th
Santa Trains	December 6/13/20th

Where

LOCATION
Hithercroft road, Wallingford, Oxfordshire OX10 0NF. Telephone (0491) 35067 (Sundays Only)
ACCESS
By Bus: South Midlands Bus Company
By Road: Wallingford is on the A329. Cholsey is on a B road off the A329
BY Rail: Cholsey / Didcot
FACILITIES
Shop, Victorian Railway Coach Coffee Shop, Museum, Model Railway, Miniature Railway, Car Parking (Habitat)
FARES (Not advised)
LOCOS
Barclay 0-4-0ST Thames, 08 Diesel 08123, Planet Diesel Walrus.

Wilson's View

This line is host to the 4247 Society, who are well on the way to be returning their eponymous ex-GWR 2-8-0T to duty. Indeed, as this is being written, the new bunker was being delivered to the site. There's coffee in a Victorian coach, a museum and a model & miniature railway on this little piece of God's Wonderful. When the whole scheme comes to fruition, the line will run between Cholsey and Moulsford station on the former GWR mainline and Wallingford, where operations are currently centred.

Cleethorpes Coast Light Railway

When
From 10.00hrs to 18.00hrs - Dusk in Winter
Daily at regular intervals from April 17th to September 13th, then Sundays only until December 20th.

What
Easter Eggstras	April 19th/20th
Lollipop Express	May 3rd/4th/24th/25th/August 30th/31st
Model Railway Exhibition	May 2nd to 4th
Festival of Transport	September 12th/13th
Santa Trains	December 6/13/20th

Where
LOCATION
Kingsway Station, Kings Road, Cleethorpes, DN35 OBY. Telephone (0472) 601871
ACCESS
By Bus: Service 17 from Pier
By Road: Kings Road is the main promenade access
By Rail: Cleethorpes
FACILITIES
Shop, Car & Coach Parking, Beach Access, Boating Lake, Nature Walk, Local Refreshments.

Wilson's View
One of the new entries for 1992, this line has been saved from almost certain doom by the efforts of two of Britain's most committed minium gauge enthusiasts, Chris Shaw and Colin Jepson. Originally the line was fourteen and a half inches, this avoided the need for a light railway order. During the past winter the line has been regauged to fifteen inches and will see steam in action this year for the first time in many years. New station buildings and a new loco shed have also been built - all this activity should see the Cleethorpes Coast joining the leading ranks of minimum gauge preservation.

Colne Valley Railway

When

Service operates: 12 noon to 5pm. 11.00am to 5pm Bank Holidays.

April	5/12/17th/26th
May	3/4/10/17/24/25/31st
June	7/14/21st-26th/28th
July	5/12/19/26/29th
August	2/5/9/12/16/19/23/26/30/31st
September	2/6/13/20/27th
October	4/6th-9th/11th
December	6/12/13/19/20th Santa Service early booking advised.

N.B. This site is open for static display from March/December. It is a must to book for rides on Santa Trains.

What

Schools Week	June 22nd to 26th
Playgroups	June 24th
Rising Fives	June 22nd/23rd
Victorian Week	October 6th to 9th
Santa Trains	December 6/12/13/19/20th

Where

LOCATION
Castle Hedingham Station, Gt. Yeldham Road, Castle Hedingham, Halstead, Essex.
Telephone (0787) 61174
ACCESS
By Bus: From Braintree, Hedingham & District Omnibuses
By Road: Off A604 between Hedingham and Great Yeldham
By Rail: Braintree (7 miles away)
FACILITIES
Shop, Large Picnic Site, Restaurant, Video Carriage, Car Park, Conducted Tours (for booked parties), Pullman Charter Hire, Educational Service (advance bookings only)
FARES
Adults 3.00 Children 1.50 OAP 2.00

Wilson's View

Based on what was once the Colne Valley and Halstead Railway, which runs from Chappel and Wakes Colne on the Great Eastern's Marks Tey-Sudbury line to Haverhill just over the Essex border in Cambridgeshire, the present railway occupies the site which was previously the Sible & Castle Hedingham Station. The CVR have taken conservation rather than preservation as their theme, and the quality of this work is complemented by some exemplary cuisine served in Pullman luxury.

Coventry Steam Railway Centre

When

No details were received from this site but contact details have been included. Intending visitors should draw their own conclusions and try to contact the line before making any visits.

Where

LOCATION
Coventry Steam Railway Centre, adjacent to Midlands Air Museum, Baginton.
ACCESS
By Bus: Services from Coventry town centre to Air Museum
By Road: A45 / A46 at Toll Bar End, on Coventry Airport perimeter
By Rail: Coventry
FACILITIES
Tea & Light Refreshments, 18 Lever Signal Box (ex Little Bowden Jct)
FARES
Admission charge 50p
LOCOS
Mazda prototype diesel electric.

Crewe Heritage Centre

When

Weekends April 17th to June 28th & after September 13th 10.30-16.00.
Daily June 29th to September 13th.

What

During the year there will be a number of special events, details in the press or phone the centre.

Where

LOCATION
Crewe Heritage Centre, North Junction Signal Box, Vernon Way, Crewe CW1 1DE.
Telephone (0270) 212130
ACCESS
By Bus: PMT, Midland Redline, North Western and C-Line services operating into Crewe bus station.
By Road: Via M6 junction 16, then A500 / A5020. AA signs in town centre.
By Rail: Crewe, then bus to town centre bus station.
FACILITIES
Buffet, Mother & Baby Room, Exhibition Hall, Period Model Railway, Small Exhibits Section, Vintage Rolls Royce Cars And Vintage Buses, Car & Coach Parking, Signal Box Access- which gives unrivalled views of services on the Chester, Manchester and West Coast mainline.
FARES
Adults 2.50 Children 1.00 Family 6.00. 1/2 price on weekday admissions.
LOCOS
Kerr-Stuart 0-4-0ST (Under restoration), Ex-BR Class 47 D1842, Class 45 D120, Class 25 D7523, John F Kennedy. The last surviving vehicles of the APT Locos from the NWCE & YNS MON Pool, 5029 Nunney Castle, 34027 Taw Valley, 4472 Flying Scotsman, 4498 Sir Nigel Gresley, 70000 Britannia, 71000 Duke of Gloucester.

Wilson's View

Just the sort of place one might expect to bump into the ghost of Webb having a whale of a time waiting for the Bowen to Cooke. Whilst he was waiting, he would be able to run an eye over the locos in the NWCE pool which hang out here when not hurtling, storming, flashing and dashing over the routes to Holyhead or Hereford. CHC - mainline locos, a signal box with a view and lots more!

Darlington Railway Museum

STANDARD GAUGE

When
09.30 to 17.00
Daily except Christmas and New Year Holidays.
(Budget cutbacks may cause the opening hours and days to be altered during 1992, to ensure that your visit will be worthwhile please phone before travelling).
Workshops run by Darlington R.P.S. open at various times & steam rides over a 1/4 mile track, enquire for the times of both of these operations.

What
Railway Carnival   September (dates to be announced).

Where
LOCATION
North Road Station, Darlington, County Durham DL3 6ST
Telephone (0325) 460532
ACCESS
By Bus: Darlington Transport/United from town centre
By Road: Off Darlington ring road on A167, 3/4 mile north of town centre.
By Rail: Darlington, or even North Road Station itself
FACILITIES
Shop, Buffet, Car & Coach Parking, Provision For Disabled.

Wilson's View
Fittingly housed in an original Stockton & Darlington structure, the museum boasts some wonderful exhibits from the splendid model of Hush Hush to the Kitching 0-6-0 Derwent, built for the S&DR in 1845. The friends of the museum run a demonstration steam service on a short length adjacent to the museum and are also well on the way to returning one of the Darlington-built BR Standard 2 Moguls to running order. This particular loco was one which was stuck in snow at Staindrop and had to be dug out by BR and the Army!

————'WESTMINSTER'————

Dean Forest Railway

STANDARD GAUGE

When
Steam Operating Days.

April	5/12/17th-20th/26th
May	2nd-4th/10/17/23rd-25th/27/31st
June	3/7/10/14/17/20/21/24/28th
July	1/5/8/12/15/19/21st-23rd/26/28th-30th
August	2/4th-6th/9/11th-13th/16/18th-20th/23/25th-27th/29th-31st
September	2/6/13/19/20/27th
October	18th
November	29th
December	5/6/12/13/19/20/27th
January	1st (1993)

Trains now run to Lydney Lakeside from 11.00am to 5pm Saturdays, Sundays & Bank Holiday Mondays.
13.00 - 17.00 on Wednesdays. The site is open for static display on non steam days.

What

Thomas Weekend	June 20th/21st & September 19th/20th
Model Railway Exhibition & Rally	October 17th/18th
Santa Trains	November 29th December 5/6/12/13/19/20th
Mince Pie Specials	December 27th & January 1st 1993.

Where
LOCATION
Norchard Steam Centre, Lydney, Gloucestershire
Telephone (0594) 843423
ACCESS
By Bus: From Lydney, National Welsh Service 24
By Road: On B4234 off A48 Chepstow/Gloucester road
By Rail: Lydney
FACILITIES
Shop, Buffet, Museum, Riverside Walk, Picnic Area, Photographic Display, Car & Coach Parking, Provision For Disabled.
LOCOS
Ex GWR 0-6-0PT 9681, Hunslet Wilbert and Peckett Uskmouth.
FARES
Steam Days: Adults 2.50 Children 1.50 OAP 2.00

Wilson's View
Now running to Lydney Lakeside, the DFR have the benefit of a country town terminus at one end and the rustic delights of the Dean Forest at the other. There is an excellent small exhibits museum at Norchard with, amongst other exhibits, a splendid example of the platform catering trolley - food for thought!

Didcot Railway Centre

STANDARD GAUGE

When

Steam Days

February	29th
March	1st, 29th
April	5th, 17th-20th, 26th
May	3rd/4th, 23rd-25th, 31st
June	7th, 14th, 20th-21st, 28th
July	5th, 12th, 19th, 26th
August	2nd,5th,9th,12th,16th,19th,23rd,26th,30th-31st
September	2nd,6th,26th-27th
October	4th,25th,31st
November	1st,29th
December	6th,13th,20th,27th-28th
January 1993	1st-3rd

Also open Saturdays & Sundays all year(except 26th December) and daily 4th April to 27th September 11.00-17.00 (dusk in Winter).

What

Special Events

Easter Steamings	17th-20th April
Spring Holiday Steaming	23rd-25th May
Midsummer Steaming	20th June (until 10pm)
Day for Disabled	5th July
Teddy Bears Picnic	12th July
Autumn Steam Gala	26th-27th September
Photographers' Evening	31st October
Santa Steamings	29th November, 6th,13th & 20th December

Where

LOCATION
Great Western Society Ltd, Didcot, Oxfordshire OX11 7NJ (adjacent BR Didcot Parkway.
Telephone (0235)817200
ACCESS
By Bus: From Oxford, South Midland service 302
By Road: On A4130 Wallingford to Didcot signed from A34 and M4 (junction 13).
By Rail: Didcot (access via station subway)
FACILITIES
Shop, Small Relics Museum, Car & Coach Parking, Buffet/Restaurant
LOCOS
Ex-GWR 0-4-2T No1466, 2-8-0 3822, 4-6-0s Nos 5029 Nunney Castle,6998 Burton Agnes Hall, 6024 King Edward 1, 2-6-2T No 6106, Ex-BR No. 71000 Duke of Gloucester, Ex-GWR railcar No.22. Also other Great Western Locomotives restored or under restoration.
FARES
From 2.70 on non-steam days to 4.50 for gala events.

Wilson's View

A fully operational Motive Power Depot, with workshops, coaling stage, turntable and all the fun of the fair. In the small exhibits museum is an area made out like a station master's office - the calendar is kept to the day. This same meticulous attention to detail runs through the whole centre, there's even a chap called Dean in charge! One non-standard item is the motor of the carriage shed traverser - a 1.3 Austin Rover Metro engine.

East Anglian Railway Museum

STANDARD GAUGE

When

Open every day 09.00 to 17.30

Steam Days:

January 1st.	March 1st.	April 5th&17th-20th
May 3/4/24/25th	June 7/21st	July 5/19th
August 2/5/12/19/26/31/31st	September 6th/9th-12th	October 3rd/4th.
November 30th	December 6/12/13/20th	

Schools Services (Diesel Hauled) May 6th June 10th & July 1st
Schools Services (Steam Hauled) June 17th & September 30th

What

Hot Dog Special	January 1st
6th Chappel Beer Festival	September 9th to 12th
Photographers Evening	October 3rd
Enthusiasts Day	October 4th
Santa Trains	November 30th & December 6/12/13/20th

Where

LOCATION
Chappel & Wakes Colne Station, Colchester, Essex CO6 2DS
Telephone (0206) 242524
ACCESS
By Bus: Halstead service from Colchester
By Road: On A604 Colchester to Cambridge road, 5 miles from A12
By Rail: Colchester or Chappel & Wakes Colne (adjacent)
FACILITIES
Shop, Buffet, Educational Service, Conducted Tours (by arrangement), Picnic Area, Car &
Coach Parking, New Heritage Centre.
FARES
Non-Steam days Adults 2.00, Child/O.A.P. 1.00, Family 5.50, Steam Days Adult 3.50, Child/
O.A.P. 2.00, Family 10.00.

Wilson's View

Vintage rolling stock, an excellent selection of items of railway architecture and the occasional main-line steam shuttle event all help to promote the East Anglian Railway Museum's annual beer festival - or is it the other way round? Whether it's beer, steam, or steam beer it's gotta be EARM.

East Lancashire Railway

STANDARD GAUGE

When

		SO.D		D		D		D		N.D
Bury	Dep	09.00	10.00	11.00	12.00	13.00	14.00	15.00	16.00	17.00
Summerseat		09.12	10.12	11.12	12.12	13.12	14.12	15.12	16.12	17.12
Ramsbottom	Arr	09.18	10.18	11.18	12.18	13.18	14.18	15.18	16.18	17.18
Ramsbottom	Dep	09.25	10.25	11.25	12.25	13.25	14.25	15.25	16.25	17.25
Irwell Vale	Dep	09.33	10.33	11.33	12.33	13.33	14.33	15.33	16.33	17.33
Rawtenstall	Arr	09.45	10.45	11.45	12.45	13.45	14.45	15.45	16.45	17.45

		SO.D		D		D		D		N.D
Rawtenstall	Dep	10.00	11.00	12.00	13.00	14.00	15.00	16.00	17.00	18.00
Irwell Vale	Dep	10.10	11.10	12.10	13.10	14.10	15.10	16.10	17.10	18.10
Ramsbottom	Arr	10.19	11.19	12.19	13.19	14.19	15.19	16.19	17.19	18.19
Ramsbottom	Dep	10.30	11.30	12.30	13.30	14.30	15.30	16.30	17.30	18.30
Summerseat		10.36	11.36	12.36	13.36	14.36	15.36	16.36	17.36	18.36
Bury	Arr	10.47	11.47	12.47	13.47	14.47	15.47	16.47	17.47	18.47

Notes: SO. Saturdays only. N. Not Sundays in January, February and March or after 27th September. D Diesel.

Services Operate:
Saturdays, Sundays & Bank Holiday Mondays from December 28th 1991, except New Year's Day 1992.

What

Big Engine Weekend	January 26th/27th
Big Engine Weekend	February 22nd/23rd
Mothers Day Special	March 29th
Diesel Weekend	June 6th/7th
Teddy Bears Picnic	August 31st. (Bank Holiday Monday).
Friends of Thomas	September
Diesel Weekend	October 3rd/4th
Santa Specials	December.

Where

LOCATION
East Lancashire Railway, Bolton Street Station, Bury, Lancashire
Telephone (061) 7647790
ACCESS
By Bus: Greater Manchester Transport, Bury service
By Road: Off Bolton Street, Bury. Bury is on the A58
By Rail: Bury (regular service from Manchester Victoria)
FACILITIES
Shop, Buffet, Museum, Vintage Bus Trips & Guided Walks, Car Parking.
LOCOS
Ex-BR STD 4 76079, J 94 0-6-0T Sir Robert Peel, RSH No1 0-6-0T, MSC No32 Gothenburg 0-6-0T, J 94 0-6-0T No193.

Wilson's View

1991 saw the opening of the Rawtenstall extension; 1992 sees work in hand on the connection to Heywood. The ELR have come a long way in a relatively short time. They've seen some interesting visiting locos and doubtless there'll be more to follow. The ELR may not qualify as one of the early pioneers of the movement but there's no doubting its place in the front ranks today.

East Somerset Railway

STANDARD GAUGE

When
Table A

						A
Cranmore	Dep	11.45	13.15	14.25	15.35	16.45
Cranmore West		11.48	13.18	14.28	15.38	16.48
Merryfield		11.52	13.22	14.32	15.42	16.52
Mendip Vale	Arr	11.57	13.27	14.37	15.47	16.57
Mendip Vale	Dep	12.05	13.35	14.45	15.55	17.05
Merryfield		12.11	13.41	14.51	16.01	17.11
Cranmore West		12.15	13.45	14.55	16.05	17.15
Cranmore	Arr	12.17	13.47	14.57	16.07	17.17

Table B

Cranmore	Dep	11.00	12.00	13.25	14.15	15.05	15.55	16.45
Cranmore West		11.03	12.03	13.28	14.18	15.08	15.58	16.48
Merryfield		11.07	12.07	13.32	14.22	15.12	16.02	16.52
Mendip Vale	Arr	11.12	12.12	13.37	14.27	15.17	16.07	16.57
Mendip Vale	Dep	11.20	12.20	13.45	14.35	15.25	16.15	17.05
Merryfield		11.26	12.26	13.51	14.41	15.31	16.21	17.11
Cranmore West		11.30	12.30	13.55	14.45	15.35	16.25	17.15
Cranmore	Arr	11.32	12.32	13.57	14.47	15.37	16.27	17.17

Table C

Cranmore	Dep	14.00	15.15	16.30
Cranmore West		14.03	15.18	16.33
Merryfield		14.07	15.22	16.37
Mendip Vale	Arr	14.12	15.27	16.42
Mendip Vale	Dep	14.20	15.35	16.50
Merryfield		14.26	15.41	16.56
Cranmore West		14.30	15.45	17.00
Cranmore	Arr	14.32	15.47	17.02

Table D

Cranmore	Dep	12.00	14.00	15.30
Cranmore West		12.03	14.03	15.33
Merryfield		12.07	14.07	15.37
Mendip Vale	Arr	12.12	14.12	15.42
Mendip Vale	Dep	12.20	14.20	15.50
Merryfield		12.26	14.26	15.56
Cranmore West		12.30	14.30	16.00
Cranmore	Arr	12.32	14.32	16.02

Notes (A) Does not run Wednesdays in June

Service Operates

Table A
Sundays — April 26th to July 12th & September 6th to 27th except May 3rd & 24th
Wednesdays — May 27th to September 2nd.
Thursdays — July 23rd to August 27th.
Fridays — April 17th.
Saturdays — April 18th, May 23rd, August 29th, October 3rd.

Table B
Sundays — April 19th, May 3rd & 24th, July 19th to August 30th & October 4th.
Mondays — April 20th, May 4th & 25th, August 31st.

Table C
Saturdays — April 25th to September 26th except May 23rd & August 29th.

Table D
Sundays — March 1st to April 12th & October 11th to November 1st.

Site open daily April to October 10.00 to 17.30, 16.00 Mondays to Fridays in April & October, Saturdays & Sundays November, December & March 10.00 to 16.00.

What

Spirit of 60's M/Cycle Rally	May 10th
David Shepherd Originals Display	June 13th/14th
Jazz Night	August 1st in shed
Vintage Commercial Vehicle Rally	July 23rd
Cranmore Village Fayre	August 31st
Enthusiasts Weekend	October 3/4th
Santa Specials	December 5/6/12/13/19/20/21/22

Where

LOCATION
Cranmore Station, Shepton Mallet, Somerset
Telephone (074) 988 417
ACCESS
By Bus: Shepton/Frome service
By Road: 3 miles out of Shepton Mallet on A361
FACILITIES
Shop, Buffet, Restaurant, Art Gallery in signal box, Picnic Area. Car Parking, Children's Play Area, Wildlife Information Centre.

Wilson's View

The East Somerset, with its `Oh so atmospheric' engine shed can now boast new shop and restaurant facilities and a freshly restored LBSCR E1. Picnic sites, a play area and a signal-box Art Gallery dedicated to the work of David Shepherd, help to ensure that there is something for everyone at ESR.

Embsay Steam Railway

STANDARD GAUGE

When

Bow Bridge	Dep		11.42	12.42	13.57	14.57	15.57	16.57
Embsay	Arr		11.45	12.45	14.00	15.00	16.00	17.00
Embsay	Dep	11.00	12.00	13.15	14.15	15.15	16.15	
Holywell Halt	Dep	11.09	12.09	13.24	14.24	15.24	16.24	
Stoneacre	Arr	11.13	12.13	13.28	14.28	15.28	16.28	
Stoneacre	Dep	11.18	12.18	13.33	14.33	15.33	16.33	
Holywell Halt	Dep	11.25	12.25	13.40	14.40	15.40	16.40	
Embsay	Arr	Passes Through						
Bow Bridge	Arr	11.37	12.37	13.52	14.52	15.52	16.52	

Bank Holiday Sundays/Mondays & Special Events

Bow Bridge	Dep	11.09	11.39	12.09	12.39	13.09	13.39
Embsay	Dep	Passes Through					
Holywell Halt	Dep	11.22	11.52	12.22	12.52	13.22	13.52
Stoneacre	Arr	11.26	11.56	12.26	12.56	13.26	13.56
Stoneacre	Dep			11.31	12.01	12.31	13.01
Holywell Halt	Dep			11.36	12.06	12.36	13.06
Embsay	Arr			11.43	12.13	12.43	13.13
Embsay	Dep	11.00	11.30	12.00	12.30	13.00	13.30
Bow Bridge	Arr	11.04	11.34	12.04	12.34	13.04	13.34

Bow Bridge	Dep	14.09	14.39	15.09	15.39	16.09	
Embsay	Dep	Passes Through				16.15	
Holywell Halt	Dep	14.22	14.52	15.22	15.52	16.24	
Stoneacre	Arr	14.26	14.56	15.26	15.56	16.28	
Stoneacre	Dep	13.31	14.01	14.31	15.01	15.31	16.01	16.33
Holywell Halt	Dep	13.36	14.06	14.36	15.06	15.36	16.06	16.38
Embsay	Arr	13.43	14.13	14.43	15.13	15.43	16.13	16.45
Embsay	Dep	14.00	14.30	15.00	15.30	16.00	
Bow Bridge	Arr	14.04	14.34	15.04	15.34	16.04	

Service Operates:
Every Sunday & Bank Holiday ,Tuesdays & Saturdays in July.
Daily Except Monday & Friday in August.
Sundays in November, December for Santa Trains. (booking recommended).

What

Mothers Day Special	March 29th
Easter Egg Specials	April 19/20th
Kiddies Day	May 4th, June 21st, July 19th
Thomas Events	May 24th/25th, August 30/31st
Festival of Steam	September 20th
Teddy Bears Picnic	August 16th
Halloween Specials	October 25th
Bonfire Night	October 31st
Santa Trains	November 22nd & every Sunday to December 20th
Family Day	January 1st 1993 (Fat Controller etc).

Where

LOCATION
Embsay Station, Embsay, Nr Skipton, North Yorkshire
Telephone (0756) 794727 / 795189.
ACCESS
By Bus: West Yorkshire Services to Skipton from Leeds, Bradford and Keighley.
By Road: Off A59 Skipton to Harrogate, road signposted to Embsay.
By Rail: Skipton
FACILITIES
Shop, Buffet, Car & Coach Parking, 10 1/4" Gauge, Line Under Construction, Picnic Site At Holywell Halt, Small Exhibits Museum, Mining Museum, Wine & Dine Trains (booking essential)
FARES
Adults 2.20 Children 1.10 unlimited travel except at peak periods, reduced fares on winter trains.
LOCOS
0-6-0ST's Wheldale, Beatrice, Primrose No2, 0-4-0 Barclay No 22 East Hetton Colliery, Diesels D2203, Ruston 887.

Wilson's View

The growth towards Bolton Abbey continues, and during last season another half mile was opened, taking the line beyond Holywell Halt on towards Draughton. This is the railway which pioneered the 'Feel of Steam' events for the blind, and its regular children's events are extremely popular. For the purists there are some excellent restorations and this year the possibility of a visit from a Mickey Mouse mogul - a sort of Disney World for Gricers.

Fairbourne Railway

When
Service Operates:
This railway is at present up for sale and it may be sold at any time, to ensure that services are in operation please phone before travelling.

The 1992 season will commence on April 17th and run until the end of October. Services will depart at regular intervals from 11.00hrs to 17.00hrs in the Summer months, July to September.

Where
LOCATION
Beach Road, Fairbourne, Gwynedd LL38 2EX. Telephone (0341) 250362.
ACCESS
By Bus: From Barmouth S28.
By Road: On A493 between Tywyn & Dolgellau.
By Rail: Fairbourne.
FACILITIES
Shop, Buffet/Restaurant, Mother & Baby Room, Birdland.
LOCOS
Yeo, Sherpa. 1

Wilsons' View
Some excellent half-size replicas, very plush rolling stock, even a fleet of authentic-looking wagons are to be found at Fairbourne. There are semaphore signals, a tunnel and, at the end of the line, a face-feeding station which has views of some of the most appealing scenery in Wales.

Ffestiniog Railway

When

Table A

Porthmadog	Dep	10.45	14.45
Ffestiniog	Arr	11.50	15.50
Ffestiniog	Dep	12.15	16.00
Porthmadog	Arr	13.15	17.00

Table D

		N.S		N.S	
Porthmadog	Dep	09.45	10.45	12.45	14.45
Ffestiniog	Arr	10.50	11.50	13.50	15.50
Ffestiniog	Dep	11.00	12.15	14.00	16.00
Porthmadog	Arr	12.00	13.25	15.05	17.00

Table B

		D		A	E	A		D
Porthmadog	Dep	09.45	10.45	11.45	12.45	13.45	14.45	15.45
Minfford		09.54	10.54	11.54	12.54	13.54	14.54	15.54
Penrhyn		10.00	11.00	12.00	13.00	14.00	15.00	16.00
Tan-y-Bwlch		10.20	11.20	12.20	13.20	14.20	15.20	16.20
Ffestiniog	Arr	10.50	11.50	12.50	13.50	14.50	15.50	16.50
Ffestiniog	Dep	11.00	12.00	13.00	14.00	15.00	16.00	17.00
Tan-y-Bwlch		11.33	12.33	13.33	14.33	15.33	16.33	17.33
Penrhyn		11.50	12.50	13.50	14.50	15.50	16.50	17.50
Minfford		11.55	12.55	13.55	14.55	15.55	16.55	17.55
Porthmadog	Arr	12.05	13.05	14.05	15.05	16.05	17.00	18.00

Table C

		D									D
Porthmadog	Dep	08.45	09.45	10.45	11.45	12.45	13.45	14.45	15.45	16.45	17.45
Minfford		08.54	09.54	10.54	11.54	12.54	13.54	14.54	15.54	16.54	17.54
Penrhyn		09.00	10.00	11.00	12.00	13.00	14.00	15.00	16.00	17.00	18.00
Tan-y-Bwlch		09.20	10.20	11.20	12.20	13.20	14.20	15.20	16.20	17.20	18.20
Ffestiniog	Arr	09.45	10.50	11.50	12.50	13.50	14.50	15.50	16.50	17.50	18.50

		D									D
Ffestiniog	Dep	10.00	11.00	12.00	13.00	14.00	15.00	16.00	17.00	18.00	19.00
Tan-y-Bwlch		10.33	11.33	12.33	13.33	14.33	15.33	16.33	17.33	18.33	19.33
Penrhyn		10.50	11.50	12.50	13.50	14.50	15.50	16.50	17.50	18.50	19.50
Minnfford		10.55	11.55	12.55	13.55	14.55	15.55	16.55	17.55	18.55	19.55
Porthmadog	Arr	11.05	12.05	13.05	14.05	15.05	16.05	17.05	18.05	19.00	20.00

Notes:
(A) Commences Monday June 29th (E) Steam hauled until June 27th then diesel service.
(N.S) Not Sundays October 5th to November 8th
(D) Diesel Service

Services Operate:
Table A. Saturdays & Sundays March 7th to 22nd, Monday to Thursday March 23rd-26th, daily December 26th to January 3rd 1993.

Table B. April 18th-21st, Monday to Saturday May 29th-July 24th & September 7th-19th, Friday to Sunday July 25th to September 6th.

Table C. May 23rd to 28th & Monday to Thursday July 25th to September 6th.

Table D. Daily March 28th to May 22nd & September 20th to November 8th, also Sundays May 29th to July 24th & September 7th to 19th.

What
Extra Services at Easter

Where
LOCATION
Ffestiniog Railway, Harbour Station, Porthmadog, Gwynedd LL49 9NF. Tel: (0766) 512340.
ACCESS
By Bus: Services from Dolgellau, Pwllheli and Caernarfon.
By Road: Porthmadog is on the A497.
By Rail: Porthmadog, Minfford, Bleanau Ffestiniog.
FACILITIES
Shop, Buffet, Museum, Car Park, Observation Coach, Nature Trail (Tan-y-Bwlch), Train Buffet.
LOCOS
FR 0-4-4-OT Merriddin Emrys, 2-4-OTT Blanche, 2-4-OTT Linda, 2-6-2T Mountaineer, FR 0-4-4-OT Earl of Merioneth, Diesel Upnor Castle.

Wilson's View
This is a very visitable railway with some interesting projects and a double and a single Fairlie - the former will be nearing completion this year. The station at Bleaneau Ffestiniog now boasts a platform canopy and improved waiting room facilities - not before time some might say, but not me of course! Probably a legend in its own lunchtime - the Ffestiniog has much to command it and, if you've never been, shame on you - the line and locos are a treat.

Forest Railroad Park

When

Daily Easter to the end of October 10.00 to 18.00. Saturdays & Sundays November to Easter 11.00 to 17.00. Last admission is 90 minutes before closing time.

What

Besides the Forest Railroad, Dobwalls Theme Park has a number of other attractions: Mr Thorburn's `Edwardian Countryside' which includes the paintings of Edward Thorburn and an authentic recreation of an Edwardian Street with shops and a tea room. There is a Swedish designed adventure playground and numerous other smaller attractions, such as `drive your own' model boats, a shooting gallery and picnic areas.

Where

LOCATION
Dobwalls Theme Park, Nr Liskeard, Cornwall. Telephone (0579) 203 25 or 211 29.
ACCESS
By Bus: No Service
By Road: Off A38 3 miles south west of Liskeard.
By Rail: Liskeard.
FACILITIES
Shop, Buffet, Restaurant. Provision For Disabled, Car & Coach Parking, Educational Service, Toddlers Play Area.
LOCOS
4-8-8-4 No 4008 William Jeffers, 4-8-4 No 818, Queen of Wyoming, 4-8-4 No 836, Queen of Nebraska, 2-8-2 No 488 General Palmer, 2-8-2 No 478 Otto Mears, 2-6-2 No 8 David Curwen, Diesels No 3008, Centennial No 108.

Wilson's View

John Southern's homage to the Sante Fe and the Union Pacific is a masterpiece of Railroading in Miniature. The Railway has the largest seven and a quarter inch gauge locomotive in the country, a replica of a UP Big Boy 4-8-8-4 Thomas Jefferson. Despite the narrow gauge, there are tressle bridges, tunnels, full colour light signalling, two completely different routes, twin and, in parts, even quadruple track. It may be in a theme park, but it sure is serious railway.

Foxfield Light Railway

STANDARD GAUGE

When

		ABC	B	A	BC	A	B	C	AB
Blythe Bridge (Caverswall Road)	Dep	12.00	13.30	14.00	14.30	15.15	15.30	16.00	16.30
Dilhorne Park	Arr	12.18	13.48	14.18	14.48	15.33	15.48	16.18	16.48
Dilhorne Park	Dep	12.25	13.55	14.25	14.55	15.40	15.55	16.25	16.55
Blythe Bridge	Arr	12.43	14.13	14.43	15.13	15.58	16.13	16.43	17.13

Notes: (A) Normal Sundays (B) Bank Holiday Sundays & Mondays (C) Bank Holiday Saturdays

Service Operates:
Easter to end of September Sundays & Bank Holiday Saturdays, Sundays & Mondays.

What

Thomas Weekend	May 2nd-4th inc
Bagnall Day	June 14th
Teddy Bears Picnic	June 28th
Silver Jubilee Gala Weekend	July 27/28th
Thomas Weekend	August 22/23rd
End of Season Gala	September 27th
Santa Trains	December 1/2/8/9/15/16/22/23rd

Santa Trains depart Blythe Bridge at: 11.00, 12.30, 14.00,15.30   Booking Essential.

Where

LOCATION
Blythe Bridge(Caverswall Road) Stoke-On-Trent. Telephone (0782)396210.
ACCESS
By Bus: From Stoke Blythe Bridge Service.
By Road: Off Old A50 South of Stoke by Blythe Bridge Level Crossing.
By Rail: Blythe Bridge.
FACILITIES
Shop, Buffet, Car & Coach Parking, Wine & Dine Service (booking essential), Museum.
FARES
Adults 2.20, Children 1.10, Family 6.00, 2 Adults & 2 Children.
LOCOS
Hawarden,Lewisham,Whiston,Wimblebury,Little Barford,possibly CPC and visiting locos for Gala day.

Wilson's View

This former colliery line, despite its origins, is a very scenic route. This year, work will be in progress to enable passenger trains to be run down Dilhorne Bank, 1 in 19, into Dilhorne Colliery Halt. There are also new developments at the Blythe Bridge site which will improve the museum and give extra covered accommodation for the growing fleet of Bagnalls, Barclays, and Pecketts. The line is well kept, well run and well worth a visit!

Opposite: Milk churns in the snow at Butterley station,
Midlands Railway Centre - another big freeze!

ABOUT 6 MILES

Gloucester & Warwickshire Railway

STANDARD GAUGE

When
Table A

		XD						YD
Toddington	Dep	11.00	12.00	13.00	14.00	15.00	16.00	17.00

Note: XD Diesel service on Saturdays except Bank Holiday Saturdays. Does not run on July 22/29th or August 5/12/17th-21st/26th.
YD Does not run Saturdays except Bank Holiday Saturdays in April and May, August 22nd/29th Diesel hauled on Saturdays Sept 26th and Oct 3rd.

Service Operates:

March	15/22/28/29th
April	4/5/11/12/17/18/19-21/25/26th
May	2-4th/9/10/16/17/23-25th/30/31st
June	6/7/13/14/20/21/27/28th
July	4/5/11/12/18/19/22/25/26/29th
August	1/2/5/8th-23rd/25/26/29/30th
September	2/5/6/12/13/19/20/26/27th
October	3/4/10/11th
November	28/29th
December	5/6/12/13/19/20/26/27th
Jan 93	1/2/3

The miniature railway will operate on:
Sundays in June July and August, also runs Bank Holiday Sundays & Mondays.

What

Schools Day	June 17th
Thomas Weekend	July 4th/5th
Teddy Bears Picnic	August 15th/16th
Extravaganza Weekend	October 10th/11th
Santa Specials	November 28th/29/December 5/6/12/13/19/20th
Mince Pie Trains	December 26th/27th
New Year Specials	January 1/2/3rd 1993

Where

LOCATION
The Railway Station, Toddington, Nr Cheltenham, Gloucestershire GL54 5DT
Telephone (0242) 621405
ACCESS
By Bus: National Bus Co service X68 Stratford to Gloucester
By Road: Off B4632 south of Broadway
By Rail: Cheltenham Spa
FACILITIES
Shop, Buffet, Museum, Car & Coach Parking and Miniature Railway
LOCOS
Ex-GWR 0-6-0PT 7752, Ex-GWR 4-6-0 5080 Defiant, 0-4-0 Peckett, 0 = 6 =0 Hunslet and 0-6-0 Bagnall.

Wilson's View

The GWR has made a great deal of progress during the past couple of years. The line has grown and continues to do so, the new station buildings at Winchcombe have created a very picturesque country halt, and a visiting loco policy has seen some of the GWR's finest in action - 5080 Defiant and 3440 City of Truro to name but two. In the next year or so the GWR will be giving bigger and more illustrious names a good run for their money, if the current progress continues.

Great Central Railway

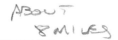

ABOUT 8 MILES (handwritten)

STANDARD GAUGE

When

		D	S	A	SG	A	SG	A	S	B	CF
Loughborough	Dep	09.30	10.00	11.00	12.00	13.00	14.00	15.00	16.00	17.00	19.30
Quorn & W'House	Arr	09.36	10.08	11.08	12.08	13.08	14.08	15.08	16.08	17.08	
Quorn & W'House	Dep	09.37	10.09	11.09	12.09	13.09	14.09	15.09	16.09	17.09	
Rothley	Arr	09.45	10.18	11.18	12.18	13.18	14.18	15.18	16.18	17.18	
Rothley	Dep	09.46	10.22	11.22	12.22	13.22	14.22	15.22	16.22	17.22	
Leicester Nth	Arr	09.55	10.32	11.32	12.32	13.32	14.32	15.32	16.32	17.32	20.34

		D	S	A	SG	A	SG	A	S	B	CF
Leicester Nth	Dep	10.10	11.10	12.10	13.10	14.10	15.10	16.10	17.10	18.10	20.54
Rothley	Arr	10.19	11.19	12.19	13.19	14.19	15.19	16.19	17.19	18.19	
Rothley	Dep	10.23	11.23	12.23	13.23	14.23	15.23	16.23	17.23	18.23	
Quorn & W'House	Arr	10.31	11.31	12.31	13.31	14.31	15.31	16.31	17.31	18.31	
Quorn & W'House	Dep	10.32	11.32	12.32	13.32	14.32	15.32	16.32	17.32	18.32	
Loughborough	Arr	10.39	11.39	12.39	13.39	14.39	15.39	16.39	17.39	18.39	21.30

Notes:
A: Runs every Sunday, Saturdays April to October & December, the 13.00hrs service runs on Sundays as The Carrillion. This incorporates a full luncheon service which must be booked.
B: Runs Saturdays April to October, Sundays March to October & Bank Holiday Mondays.
CF: Charnwood Forester Wine and Dine service runs Saturdays throughout the year and Wednesday evenings May to September. Booking is essential.
D: Diesel service with reduced fares runs Saturdays April to October & Saturdays in December. N.B on special events this service may be steam hauled and ordinary fares will apply.
S&SG: These services run every Saturday and Sunday throughout the year and every weekday from May 4th to September 30th and from December 14th to 31st inc. Those marked SG include a griddle, serving hot and cold lunches & afternoon teas.

What

Butler Henderson Farewell	Monday February 24th
Steam Galas	February 22/23rd, June 13/14th, October 3/4th

Where

LOCATION

Loughborough Central Station, Great Central Road, Loughborough, Leicestershire LE11 1SS
Telephone (0509) 230726

ACCESS

By Bus: Trent & Midland Red services from Nottingham to Loughborough. Ring road service from Leicester Midland to Leicester Nth.

By Road: Loughborough Central is off A6 just south of town centre. Leicester North station is adjacent to Leicester ring road.

By Rail: Loughborough Midland/Leicester Midland.

FACILITIES

Shop, Buffet, Museum, Car Parking, Charnwood Forester Wine & Dine Service.

LOCOS

Ex-SR 4-6-2 35005 Canadian Pacific, Ex-S.R. 4-4-0 30926 Repton, Ex-LMS 5XP 4-6-0 5593 Kolhapur, Ex-GWR 4-6-0 6990 Witherslack Hall, Ex-GWR 4-6-0 7029 Clun Castle, Ex-GCR 4-4-0 506 Butler Henderson, Ex-GWR 2-8-0T 5224, Ex-LNER 0-6-0T J94 68009, Ex-LNER Y7 0-4-0T 68088, Industrial 0-6-0T 7597

There are also likely visiting locos at special events during the year.

Wilson's View

The railway of the 1990's, the GCR have made very substantial progress in the last two years. A new terminus at Leicester, just off the ring road, the construction of a twin-track under way, and now a home for the Tyseley team and loco fleet. The motive power line-up is mouthwatering with a Schools, Channel Packet, Castle, Hall, Director, Jubilee and a West Country, soon to joined by a B1, 9F and a N2. There's also a GWR 2-8-0T and a Y7 with an 8F, another West Country and yet another Channel Packet still in the pipeline - PHEW!

Groudle Glen Railway

NARROW GAUGE

When

Groudle Glen Station to Headland Terminus.
Trains depart at regular intervals between 11.00-16.30
An evening service runs on Wednesdays in July and August between 19.00-21.00.

Services Operate:

Easter Sunday & Monday	April 19th/20th
Sundays	May 24th to September 27th
Bank Holiday Mondays	May 25th & August 31st
Wednesday Evenings	July & August

What

Santa Trains	December 13th/20th 11.00-15.30
Mince Pie Trains	December 26th 12 noon-15.30

Where

LOCATION

Near Douglas, Isle of Man. Postal address: 19 Ballabrooie Grove, Douglas, IOM

Telephone (evenings only) (0624) 622138
ACCESS
By Sea: Via Isle of Man Steam Packet Co.
By Road: 2 miles from Douglas on Laxey road, adjacent to Groudle Glen hotel.
By Tram: Manx Electric Tram from Douglas
FACILITIES
Gift Shop, Guides Available
LOCO
Sea Lion (Bagnall), built 1896

Wilson's View

A little piece of Victorian leisure history, this line carried tourists to a sea-life marina created in a Manx cove. The line has one of the original locos, the Sea Lion. Built in 1896, the Sea Lion returned to active service in 1987 after repairs and restoration by apprentices at BNFL. The Groudle Glen railway's eventual aim is to run a service to the original terminus at Sea Lion rocks. Currently, the line terminates at Headland.

Gwili Railway

ABOUT 2 MILES

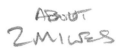

STANDARD GAUGE

When

A

| Bronwydd Arms | Dep | 11.00 | 12.00 | 13.30 | 14.40 | 15.30 | 16.30 | 17.30 |

Notes: (A) Runs Bank Holiday Sundays and Mondays only.

Service Operates:

April	17th to 22nd
May	3/4/10/17/21st. to 31st
June	3/7/10/14/17/21/24/28th
July	1/4/5/8/11/12/15/18/19th
Daily	From July 22nd to September 2nd
September	6/13/20/27th
October	18/21/24/25th
December	13/19th to 23rd. Last train in December runs at 15.00.

What

Taff Vale coach in service Bank Holiday Sundays and Mondays, (except Christmas), Sundays and Wednesdays in July & August and on October 25th.

Easter Egg Hunt	April 17th/18th
Teddy Bear Weekend	July 4th/5th
Autumn Steam Gala	October 24th & 25th (special timetable)
Santa Trains	December 13th/19th to 23rd

Where

LOCATION

Bronwydd Arms Station, Bronwydd Arms, Carmarthen, Dyfed

Telephone (0267) 230666 Operating days only (0656) 732176 Booking Office.

ACCESS

By Bus: From Carmarthen Davies Bros (Not Sundays or Bank Holidays).

By Road: On A484 3 miles north of Carmarthen.

By Rail: Carmarthen.

FACILITIES

Shop, Buffet, Car Park, Picnic Site, Working Signal Box.

FARES

Adults 2.50, Children/O.A.P./UB 40 1.25, Family 6.50 (except December services).

Fares give unlimited rides except on special event days.

LOCOS

Rosyth No 1, Olwen and 0-6-0 Hunslet Austerity, 71516, visiting locos to be arranged.

Wilson's View

Deep in the heart of south west Wales, the Gwili Railway have done a marvellous job of restoration on the Bronwydd Arms signal box and station. They have also restored a Taff Vale coach, which won the judges' commendation in the ARPS coaching stock awards. The latest coach restoration is a six-wheel, wooden-bodied GWR coach and, whilst on the subject of wood, the upper section of the line follows the wooded banks of the Gwili. Trés rustic!

Hunsbury Hill Industrial Museum

STANDARD GAUGE

When

Museum open every Sunday.

Railway operates Easter Sunday & Monday, Spring Bank Holiday Sunday & Monday, then every Sunday until the end of September. Also open August Bank Holiday Monday.

What

Special events in September (For details contact Railway).

Where

LOCATION

Hunsbury Hill Ironstone Railway Museum, Camp Hill, Northampton. Postal and phone contact (evenings only), The General Manager, 9 High Street, Hallaton, Market Harborough, Leicestershire LE16 8UD. Telephone (085889) 216.

ACCESS

By Bus: Services 24/25/26 to Camp Hill from Greyfriars Bus Station.

By Road: Between A43 and Northampton ring road.

By Rail: Northampton.

FACILITIES

Shop, Buffet, Photographic Displays, Models, Facilities for Disabled, Car & Coach parking, Set in Country Park.

FARES

Museum admission Adult 30p, children 15p, Train Fares, Adults 90p children 50p return. (1991 dates, 1992 not advised).

LOCOS

Ex-Ironstone railway industrial types dating from 1883 to 1963.

Wilson's View

This two mile standard gauge line is laid out in what was an ironstone quarry, now a nature reserve. The museum depicts the life of a working Ironstone quarry through a series of photographic displays and numerous artefacts. It is possible to visit either the museum or the railway, but it is recommended that you visit both. The very modest admission charges ensure that everyone should be able to enjoy both aspects.

Isfield Steam Railway

STANDARD GAUGE

When

No details were received from this site but contact details have been included. Intending visitors should draw their own conclusions and try to contact the line before making any visits.

Where

LOCATION

Station House, Isfield Station, Nr Uckfield, Sussex TN22 5XB.

Telephone (082575) 515.

ACCESS

By Road: Off A26 Uckfield/Lewes Road.

By Rail: Lewes, Uckfield.

FACILITIES

Shop, Buffet, Car & Coach Parking, Charter Train Service, Wine & Dine.

LOCOS

0-4-0ST Barclay Annie. 0-6-0ST, Hunslet 0-6-0ST 68012, class 12 diesel.

FARES

Site admission adults 2.00, children/O.A.P. 1.00 all train rides free.

Wilson's View

This line, with its prize-winning station at Isfield, has been on sale for much of 1991, and various consortia are involved in bidding for the railway. This does not, however, prevent anyone from making a visit to what must be one of the tidiest railway sites in Britain.

Isle of Man Steam Railway

NARROW GAUGE

When

		A	C	A	A	C	B	C
Douglas	Dep	10.10	10.50	11.45	14.10	15.55	16.10	16.55
Port Soderick		10.24	11.08	11.59	14.24	16.08	16.24	17.08
Santon R)		10.34	11.18	12.09	14.34	16.18	16.34	17.18
Ballasalla		10.45	11.30	12.20	14.45	16.30	16.45	17.30
Castletown		10.53	11.38	12.28	14.53	16.37	16.53	17.37
Ballabeg (R)		10.58	11.44	12.34	14.58	16.43	16.58	17.43
Colby		11.03	11.48	12.38	15.03	16.48	17.03	17.48
Level (R)		11.07	11.52	12.42	15.07	16.52	17.07	17.52
Port St Mary		11.12	11.57	12.47	15.12	16.57	17.12	17.57
Port Erin	Arr	11.15	12.00	12.50	15.15	17.00	17.15	18.00

		A	A	A	C	A	C
Port Erin	Dep	10.15	12.05	14.15	15.15	16.15	17.15
Port St Mary		10.19	12.09	14.19	15.19	16.19	17.19
Level (R)		10.24	12.14	14.24	15.24	16.24	17.24
Colby		10.27	12.17	14.27	15.27	16.27	17.27
Ballabeg (R)		10.31	12.21	14.31	15.31	16.31	17.31
Castletown		10.38	12.28	14.38	15.38	16.38	17.38
Ballasalla		10.45	12.35	14.45	15.45	16.45	17.45
Santon R)		10.58	12.45	14.58	15.58	16.58	17.58
Port Soderick		11.07	12.55	15.07	16.07	17.07	18.07
Douglas	Arr	11.20	13.10	15.20	16.20	17.20	18.20

Notes: A. Runs daily April 17th to September 27th.
B. Runs daily except Mondays to Thursdays July 6th to August 31st.
C. Runs July 6th to August 31st Monday to Thursday only.

(R) Request stop passengers wishing to alight must give clear indication to the guard, those wishing to board at these stations should give a clear signal to the driver.

What

Enthusiast Weekend   May 23rd to 25th
On one of these days there will be special photo run pasts-phone for details.

Where
LOCATION
Douglas Station, Douglas I.O.M.
Telephone (0624) 673623 or 663366
ACCESS
By Bus: I.O.M. Transport services.
By Road: Car Ferry from Liverpool or Heysham.
By Rail: Via Liverpool & I.O.M. Ferry or Heysham.
FACILITIES
Shop, Museum(Port Erin), Buffet, Special Bus Connection with Manx Electric Railway, Car Parking, Provision for Disabled.
LOCOS
I.O.M. Railways No4 Loch, No11 Maitland, No12 Hutchinson, No13 Kissak.
FARES
Douglas to Castletown 3.30, to Port Erin 4.25, Adult return, 1/2 fare for children 5-15 years.
Fares are those of 1991-1992 fares not advised.

Wilson's View
A magnificent piece of Victoriana, still in full operational order. The three-foot gauge Isle of Man Railway, which once ran to all the major towns on the Island, now serves the towns between Douglas and Port Erin. Though the management of the railway is in the hands of the Council, the responsible officials are true supporters of steam traction and the line. Its infrastructure, rolling stock and locomotives are a credit to the men and women who operate the railway - no visitor to the IOM should miss a journey on this aspect of the island's transport network.

Isle of Mull Railway

MINIMUM GAUGE

When
Easter Sunday April 19th

Torosay Castle	Dep	10.40	14.30	16.30	Craignure Dep		11.15	15.40	17.00

Easter, Early & Late Season
April 16/18/21/23/25th Daily April 27th to May 24th & September 5th to October 10th

Torosay Castle	Dep	10.40	12.10	14.10P	14.50Q	16.10
Craignure	Dep	11.15	13.15	14.30Q	15.10P	16.45

High Season Mondays to Fridays May 25th to September 4th

Torosay Castle	Dep	10.45	11.35	11.50X	12.10	12.55	14.00
Craignure	Dep	11.10	11.20	11.50X	12.30	13.10	13.30

Torosay Castle	Dep	14.15	15.05	15.40	16.10	16.20	17.30Y
Craignure	Dep	14.20	15.10	15.25	15.55	16.35	17.00

High Season Saturdays & Sundays May 30th to August 30th

Torosay Castle	Dep	10.45	12.10	14.10	14.50	16.10	17.30Z
Craignure	Dep	11.15	13.15	14.30	15.15	16.45	

Notes:
P Saturdays 18th & 25th April only then from April 27th as advertised.
Q Runs May 11th to 24th & September 5th to 19th only.
X Commences July 6th.
Y Runs May 25th to 28th then from June 15th Fridays excepted.
Z Runs June 20th to August 30th.

Where

LOCATION
Mull Rail, Craignure (Old Pier) Station, Craignure, Isle of Mull, Argyll PA65 6AY.
Telephone (06802) 494, Out of season (0680) 300389 or 300472.
ACCESS
Via Oban: Cal/Mac ferries to Mull
Via Fort William: Lochaline Fishnish Ferry.
FACILITIES
Car Park, Castle & Gardens, Picnic Site, Charter Trains Available, Ferry Connection with
Through Booking Facility From Cal/Mac in Oban.
FARES
Adult single 1.20 Return 1.75, Child single .90 Return 1.20, Family single 3.30 Return 4.70.

Wilson's View

This purpose-built line is the only one on any of the Scottish islands, and it provides a
transport link between the Ferry Terminal and the Castle at Torosay, the gardens of which
are open to public inspection. The services connect with the ferries and you can make
through bookings. There cannot be many ferries anywhere that connect with a ten and a
quarter inch gauge railway. The motive power is a Marsh-built 2-6-4T, and there is also an
Atlantic built by Curwen in 1948 and modified by Alcock.

Isle of Wight Steam Railway

STANDARD GAUGE

When
Table A

Smallbrook Jct	Dep	-	10.15	11.00	11.45	12.30	13.45	14.30	15.15	16.00	16.45
Haven Street	Arr	-	10.25	11.10	11.55	12.40	13.55	14.40	15.25	16.10	16.55
Haven Street	Dep	-	10.27	11.12	11.57	12.42	13.57	14.42	15.27	16.12	16.57
Wootton	Arr	-	10.32	11.17	12.02	12.47	14.02	14.47	15.32	16.17	17.02
Wootton	Dep	-	10.36	11.21	12.06	12.51	14.06	14.51	15.36	16.21	17.06
Haven Street	Arr	-	10.41	11.26	12.11	12.56	14.11	14.56	15.41	16.26	17.11
Haven Street	Dep	09.59	10.44	11.29	12.14	13.29	14.14	14.59	15.44	16.29	-
Smallbrook Jct	Arr	10.09	10.54	11.39	12.24	13.39	14.24	15.09	15.54	16.39	-

Table B

Smallbrook Jct	Dep	-	-	10.15	10.45	11.15	11.45	12.15	12.45
Havenstreet	Arr	-	-	10.25	10.55	11.25	11.55	12.25	12.55
Havenstreet	Dep	-	-	10.30	11.00	11.30	12.00	12.30	13.10
Wootton	Arr	-	-	10.35	11.05	11.35	12.05	12.35	13.15
Wootton	Dep	-	-	10.40	11.10	11.40	12.10	12.40	13.20
Havenstreet	Arr	-	-	10.45	11.15	11.45	12.15	12.45	13.25
Havenstreet	Dep	10.00	10.30	11.00	11.30	12.00	12.30	13.20	14.00
Smallbrook Jct	Arr	10.10	10.40	11.10	11.40	12.10	12.40	13.30	14.10

Smallbrook Jct	Dep	13.45	14.15	14.45	15.15	15.45	16.15	16.45	17.15
Haven Street	Arr	13.55	14.25	14.55	15.25	15.55	16.25	16.55	17.25
Haven Street	Dep	14.00	14.30	15.00	15.30	16.00	16.30	17.00	-
Wootton	Arr	14.05	14.35	15.05	15.35	16.05	16.35	17.05	-
Wootton	Dep	14.10	14.40	15.10	15.40	16.10	16.40	17.10	-
Haven Street	Arr	14.15	14.45	15.15	15.45	16.15	16.45	17.15	-
Haven Street	Dep	14.30	15.00	15.30	16.00	16.30	17.00	-	-
Smallbrook Jct	Arr	14.40	15.10	15.40	16.10	16.40	17.10	-	-

Service Operates:

Table A	March	26/29th
	April	2/5/9/12/16/17/21st-23rd/26/30th
	May	5th-7th/10/13/14/17/20/21/26th-28th
	June	Sundays & Tuesday to Thursday inclusive
	July	As June until 24th
	September	As June and July until 30th also Friday 4th
	October	Sundays and Thursdays until 29th
	December	13/20/26th
Table B	April	19th/20th
	May	3/4/24/25th
	July	Daily from 26th except Saturdays
	August	Daily except Saturdays. NB Services do run August 29th

On non operating days May to September the Haven Street site is open to visitors.

What

Summer Steam	August 28th to 31st
Santa Trains	December 13/20th
Mince Pie Trains	December 26th

Where

LOCATION
Haven Street Station, Ryde, Isle of Wight PO33 4DS. Telephone (0983) 882204.
ACCESS
By Bus: From Ryde Southern Vectis Services 3/43.
By Road: On By Road off A3055.
By Rail: Ryde Esplanade.
FACILITIES
Shop, Buffet, Museum, Car & Coach Parking (Haven Street).
FARES
3rd class adult 3.00, child 2.00, family 2 + 4 10.00. On the extended line the fares become 3rd class adult 4.00, child 3.00 family 2 + 4 14.00, reduced rates for parties ten and over.
LOCOS
Ex-LBSCR Terriers as I.W.C. No 11, F.Y.N. No 2, W24 Calbourne, Barclay 38 Ajax, Hawthorne Leslie 37 Invincible.

Wilson's View

Now running from Haven Street to Smallbrook Junction, the Isle of Wight Railway has consolidated its position as one of the leading lines in the South of England. There is very much a flavour of the old Southern Railway about the operations, and the island's own railways are not forgotten, with locos in the numbers and livery of both the Isle of Wight Central Railway and those of the Freshwater Yarmouth and Newport. The Southern is represented by that class most associated with the island in the last years of steam - the Adams O2s.

Keighley & Worth Valley Railway

STANDARD GAUGE

When

Table A

		D	D	R	R	R	R	R
Oxenhope	Dep	09.20	10.35	11.10	12.30	13.50	15.20	16.45
Haworth	Dep	09.26	10.40	11.16	12.36	13.56	15.26	16.51
Oakworth	Dep	09.29	10.43	11.19	12.39	13.59	15.29	16.54
Damems		All Trains Stop On Request						
Ingrow West	Dep	09.34	10.48	11.25	12.45	14.05	15.35	17.00
Keighley	Arr	09.45	10.55	11.35	12.55	14.15	15.45	17.10

		D	D	R	R	R	R	
Keighley	Dep	10.05	11.15	11.50	13.10	14.35	16.05	17.25
Ingrow West	Dep	10.09	11.19	11.54	13.14	14.39	16.09	17.29
Damems		All Trains Stop On Request						
Oakworth	Dep	10.15	11.25	12.03	13.23	14.48	16.18	17.38
Haworth	Dep	10.20	11.30	12.08	13.28	14.53	16.23	17.43
Oxenhope	Arr	10.26	11.36	12.15	13.35	15.00	16.30	17.50

Table B

Oxenhope	Dep	11.40	13.05	14.25	15.45	Keighley	Dep	12.25	13.45	15.05	16.25
Haworth	Dep	11.46	13.11	14.31	15.51	Ingrow West	Dep	12.29	13.49	15.09	16.29
Oakworth	Dep	11.49	13.14	14.34	15.54	Damems		Request Stop			
Damems		Request Stop				Oakworth	Dep	12.38	13.58	15.18	16.38
Ingrow West	Dep	11.55	13.20	14.40	16.00	Haworth	Dep	12.43	14.03	15.23	16.43
Keighley	Arr	12.05	13.30	14.50	16.10	Oxenhope	Arr	12.50	14.10	15.30	16.50

Table C

Oxenhope	Dep	09.20	10.25	11.30	12.35	13.45	14.55	16.05
Haworth	Dep	09.25	10.30	11.35	12.40	13.50	15.00	16.10
Oakworth	Dep	09.28	10.33	11.38	12.43	13.53	15.03	16.13
Damems	R	09.32	10.38	11.43	12.48	13.58	15.08	16.18
Ingrow West	Dep	09.34	10.40	11.45	12.50	14.00	15.10	16.20
Keighley	Arr	09.45	10.45	11.50	12.55	14.05	15.15	16.25

Keighley	Dep	09.55	11.00	12.05	13.15	14.25	15.35	16.45
Ingrow West	Dep	09.59	11.04	12.09	13.19	14.29	15.39	16.49
Damems	R	10.01	11.06	12.11	13.21	14.31	15.41	16.51
Oakworth	Dep	10.04	11.09	12.17	13.27	14.37	15.47	16.54
Haworth	Dep	10.10	11.15	12.22	13.32	14.42	15.52	17.00
Oxenhope	Arr	10.15	11.20	12.27	13.37	14.47	15.57	17.05

Table D

		D	D		RD/S		R		R		R	
Oxenhope	Dep	09.20	10.25	11.00	11.45	12.30	13.15	14.00	14.45	15.30	16.15	17.00	17.45
Haworth	Dep	09.26	10.30	11.07	11.56	12.37	13.22	14.07	14.52	15.37	16.22	17.07	17.52
Oakworth	Dep	09.29	10.33	11.11	11.59	12.40	13.26	14.11	14.56	15.41	16.26	17.11	17.56
Damems	R	09.32	10.36	11.15	12.02	12.43	13.30	14.15	15.00	15.45	16.30	17.15	18.00
Ingrow W.	Dep	09.36	10.40	11.19	12.05	12.46	13.34	14.19	15.04	15.49	16.34	17.19	18.04
Keighley	Arr	09.45	10.45	11.25	12.15	12.56	13.40	14.25	15.10	15.55	16.40	17.25	18.10

		D	D		RD/S	R		R		R		
Keighley	Dep	09.55	11.00	11.50	12.30	13.15	14.00	14.45	15.30	16.15	17.00	17.45	18.30
Ingrow W.	Dep	09.59	11.05	11.56	12.35	13.21	14.06	14.51	15.36	16.21	17.06	17.51	18.35
Damems	R	10.01	11.08	11.59	12.38	13.24	14.10	14.55	15.40	16.25	17.10	17.55	18.38
Oakworth	Dep	10.05	11.17	12.05	12.47	13.32	14.17	15.02	15.47	16.32	17.17	18.02	18.48
Haworth	Dep	10.10	11.22	12.10	12.50	13.37	14.22	15.07	15.52	16.37	17.22	18.07	18.53
Oxenhope	Arr	10.16	11.30	12.17	T	13.42	14.27	15.12	15.57	16.42	17.27	18.12	18.58

Table E

Oxenhope	Dep	11.50	13.20	14.50	16.20	17.40
Haworth	Dep	11.56	13.26	14.56	16.26	17.45 Arr (Terminates)
Oakworth	Dep	11.59	13.29	14.59	16.29	
Damems	R	12.02	13.32	15.02	16.32	
Ingrow West	Dep	12.05	13.35	15.05	16.35	
Keighley	Arr	12.15	13.45	15.15	16.45	
Keighley	Dep	12.35	14.05	15.35	17.05	
Ingrow West	Dep	12.39	14.09	15.39	17.09	
Damems	R	12.41	14.11	15.41	17.11	
Oakworth	Dep	12.48	14.18	15.48	17.18	
Haworth	Dep	12.53	14.23	15.53	17.23	
Oxenhope	Arr	13.00	14.30	16.00	17.30	

Table A. Operates
Saturdays February 29th to October 31st (except April 4th & 18th). Sundays March 1st to May 17th (except April 5th/19th & May 3rd) & October 4th to 25th.

Table B. Operates
Sundays December 29th 1991 to February 23rd also December 26/27/30/31st 1991 and January 1st 1992.

Table C. Operates
Saturdays only diesel service. December 28th 1991 to February 22nd 1992.

Table D Operates
Sundays May 24th to September 27th also Good Friday to Easter Tuesday, May Day Bank Holiday Sunday & Monday and Spring and August Bank Holiday Mondays

Table E Operates
Mondays to Fridays June 22nd to September 4th (except Bank Holiday Monday August 31st). Also Easter week 22nd to 24th April and Spring Bank Holiday week May 26th to 29th.

Notes: D Diesel Hauled. RD/S Normally Diesel Hauled except on Bank Holidays. R Buffet Service T Terminates.

What

Enthusiasts Weekend	April 4/5th
Santa Trains	December 5/6/12/13/19/20th (Booking Essential)
Steam Carol Service	(Details Autumn 91)

Special events throughout the year to celebrate the 125th Anniversary of the Worth Valley Line opened in 1867.

Where

LOCATION
Haworth Station, Haworth, Nr. Keighley, West Yorkshire.
Telephone (0535) 645214.
ACCESS
By Bus: West Yorkshire Services from Leeds or Bradford to Keighley or Haworth 665,666,667,668/669,670.
By Road: Off A629 Keighley/Halifax Road.
By Rail: B.R. Keighley adjoining the Keighley & Worth valley railway.
FACILITIES
Shop, Buffet, Car & Coach Parking, Museum (Oxenhope), Pullman Wine & Dine(Booking essential), B.R. Connecting Services.

FARES
Adult full line 4.00, Family 10.00, Day Rover 5.00, Children & O.A.P.'s half fare.
LOCOS
Ex-SR 4-6-2 34092 City of Wells, Ex-BR 4-6-0 75079, Ex-BR 2-6-0 78022, Ex-LMS 0-6-0T
47279, Ex-Swedish Railways W.D. 2-8-0 1931 EX-USATC 2-8-0 Big Jim, Ex-Haydock Foundry
0-6-0WT Bellerophon, Ex-LMR 0-6-0T NO 118 Brussels, Ex-SR USA Dock Tank 30072
Ex-LMS 2-8-0 48431, Ex-LMS 4-6-0 45596 Bahamas, Ex-LNWR 0-6-2 NO 1054 Coal Tank,
Barclay 0-4-0 Tiny, Hudswell Clarke 0-6-0 Nunlow, visiting locos and locos in the Oxenhope
Museum.

Wilson's View

The last twenty odd years have seen the Worth Valley progress from weed-strewn ramshackle branchline to become one of Britian's best-known and well-ordered Preserved Railways. Its delightful stations have featured in TV gardening programmes and won numerous 'Best Kept Station' awards. The M.P.D have turned out some super locos, including the gricers' favourite 34092 City of Wells. They are currently working to produce a Dub Dee - whoopee! Not the longest line in preservation, but they've got an enormous amount packed into their five and a half miles.

Kent & East Sussex Railway

STANDARD GAUGE

When

Table A

	H	V	H	V	H
Tenterden Dep	11.00	12.00	13.00	14.00	15.00
Rolvenden Dep	R	R	R	R	R
Wittersham	R	R	R	R	R
Northiam Arr	11.32	12.32	13.32	14.32	15.32
Northiam Dep	11.45	12.45	13.45	14.45	15.45
Wittersham	R	R	R	R	R
Rolvenden Dep	R	R	R	R	R
Tenterden Arr	12.23	13.23	14.23	15.23	16.23

Table B

			H		H	H
Tenterden Dep	10.30	12.00	13.00	14.00	15.00	16.30
Rolvenden Dep	R	R	R	R	R	R
Wittersham	R	R	R	R	R	R
Northiam Arr	11.02	12.32	13.32	14.32	15.32	17.02
Northiam Dep	11.17	12.47	13.47	14.47	15.47	17.17
Wittersham	R	R	R	R	R	R
Rolvenden Dep	R	R	R	R	R	R
Tenterden Arr	11.50	13.20	14.20	15.20	16.20	17.50

Table C

		V		H		V	H	V	H
Tenterden Dep	10.30	11.30	12.00	13.00	14.00	14.30	15.00	16.00	16.30
Rolvenden Dep	R	R	R	R	R	R	R	R	R
Wittersham Dep	R	R	R	R	R	R	R	R	R
Northiam Arr	11.02	12.00	12.32	13.32	14.32	15.00	15.32	16.30	17.02
Northiam Dep	11.17	12.11	12.47	13.47	14.47	15.11	15.47	16.41	17.17
Wittersham Dep	R	R	R	R	R	R	R	R	R
Rolvenden Dep	R	R	R	R	R	R	R	R	R
Tenterden Arr	11.50	12.40	13.20	14.20	15.20	15.40	16.20	17.10	17.50

Table D

Tenterden	Dep	10.45	12.15	14.30	16.00
Rolvenden	Dep	R	R	R	R
Wittersham	Dep	R	R	R	R
Northiam	Arr	11.17	12.47	15.02	16.32
Northiam	Dep	11.30	13.00	15.15	16.00
Wittersham	Dep	R	R	R	R
Rolvenden	Dep	R	R	R	R
Tenterden	Arr	12.03	13.33	15.48	17.18

Notes:
V Victorian Train. H indicates carriage adapted for handicapped.

Services Operate:
Table A   January 1st and every Sunday until March 22nd, Saturdays & Sundays November 1st to 28th then December 26th to 28th.
Table B   March 29th, April 4/5/11/12/25/26, May 2/9/10/16/17/23/26th to 31st, June 6/7/13/14/20/21, Saturdays in July, Sundays & Bank Holidays excepted in August, September 1st to 6th/12/13/26/27th, Saturdays & Sundays in October.
Table C   April 17th to 20th, May 3/4th/24/25th, June 27/28th, Sundays July August and Bank Holiday Monday, September 19/20th.
Table D   April 21st to 24th, Wednesdays & Thursdays in June, Monday to Friday in July, September 9/10/16/17/23/24/30th.

What

Thomas Event	June 27/28th
Good Old Days	September 19/20th
Santa Trains	November 29th, December 5/6/12/13/19th to 24th

Santa Trains should be booked, bookings commence August.

Where

LOCATION
Tenterden Town Station. Tenterden, Kent TN30 6HE. Tel: (05806) 2943. Office (05806) 5155.
ACCESS
By Bus: Maidstone/Headcorn Service 400/401/404 from Canterbury or Ashford service 340 from Hastings or Northiam.
By Road: On A28 Ashford/Hastings road Northiam is on A268 at jct with A28.
By Rail: Headcorn and Ashford or Hastings for Northiam.
FACILITIES
Shop, Buffet/Restaurant, Provision for Disabled, Car Parking, Museum (Station Road), Picnic Site, Children's Play Area.
LOCOS
A1X No10 Sutton, P1556, USA 30065 Maunsell, Austerities Nos 24 William H Austen, 25 Northiam, 26 Linda.
FARES
Not advised.

Wilson's View

This line, which once connected Robertsbridge with Headcorn, now runs between Tenterden and Northiam, effectively the centre section of the original route. The KESR will eventually run as far as Bodiam, where, if memory serves, there is a castle - no, not a 4 cyl 4-6-0, the bricks-and-mortar type! Motive power has a distinctly Southern flavour, tinged with ex-industrials; the rolling stock, which forms the KESR's vintage train, also has the Southern look about it. However, as the railway are quick to point out, this line was never part of the Southern, being one of Britain's many private light railways.

Kirklees Light Railway

NARROW GAUGE

When

Saturdays & Sundays throughout the year, daily from Whitsun to end of September. It is also possible that there will be some services on weekdays between Easter and Whitsun, intending travellers should check between these dates.

Services will operate at frequent intervals between 10.30hrs & 17.00hrs.

What

Extension of the running line will occur during 1992 and any special events will be advertised in the local press.

Where

LOCATION
Kirklees Light Railway, Clayton West Station, Clayton West, Huddersfield HD8 9PE
Telephone (0484) 865727
ACCESS
By Bus: From Huddersfield or Wakefield, Yorkshire Rider Services.
By Road: On the A636 just east of Denby Dale.
By Rail: Denby Dale, Huddersfield, Wakefield.
FACILITIES
Car & Coach Parking, Snacks, Shop & Exhibition Centre (Planned).
LOCOS
2-6-2T Fox, 0-6-4ST Badger.

Wilson's View

This 15" gauge line is built on the trackbed of the former Lancashire and Yorkshire Railway route from Clayton West to the Huddersfield-Penistone route, indeed over the next two years the aim is to reconnect with services on the Penistone-Huddersfield route at Clayton West Junction, where a new halt will be provided. The current operation runs over one mile of the three and a half mile line, though further extensions are in the pipeline for 1992. The rolling stock and locomotives have been built in the railway's own workshops, specifically for the line. There are also proposals to site a Mill Engine museum here at the Kirklees Light Railway and there are also plans to create craft workshops in a former railway goods warehouse adjacent to the station at Clayton West.

Lakeside & Haverthwaite Railway

STANDARD GAUGE

When
Table A

							B
Haverthwaite	Dep	10.40	11.45	12.55	14.00	15.05	16.20
Newby Bridge		10.52	11.57	13.07	14.12	15.17	16.32
Lakeside	Arr	10.58	12.03	13.13	14.18	15.23	16.38
Windermere Steamer	Arr	11.10	12.05	-	14.20	15.25	17.10
	Dep	11.15	12.15	-	14.25	15.35	-
							B
Lakeside	Dep	11.15	12.20	13.25	14.30	15.40	17.15
Newby Bridge		11.21	12.26	13.31	14.36	15.46	17.21
Haverthwaite	Arr	11.33	12.38	13.43	14.48	15.58	17.33

Table B

								A
Haverthwaite	Dep	10.40	11.45	13.00	14.05	15.10	16.15	17.20
Newby Bridge	Dep	10.52	11.57	13.12	14.17	15.22	16.27	17.32
Lakeside	Arr	10.58	12.03	13.18	14.23	15.28	16.33	17.38
Windermere Steamer	Arr	11.05	12.20	13.25	14.30	15.35	16.40	17.40C
	Dep	11.20	12.30	13.35	14.40	15.45	16.50	17.45C
								A
Lakeside	Dep	11.15	12.30	13.35	14.40	15.45	16.50	17.20
Newby Bridge	Dep	11.21	12.36	13.41	14.46	15.51	16.56	17.26
Haverthwaite	Arr	11.33	12.48	13.53	14.58	16.03	17.08	18.06

Note: A Operates May 24th to 31st & July 19th to September 6th & may be diesel hauled
C Sails on the same dates on which A runs

Service Operates:
Table A   Daily April 11th to April 26th & September 28th to November 1st
Table B   Daily May 2nd to September 27th
All trains connect with Windermere cruise boats in their arrival and departure times.

Where
LOCATION
Haverthwaite Station, Nr Ulverstone, Cumbria LA12 8AL.
Telephone (05395) 31594.
ACCESS
By Bus: C.M.S. Service from Windermere.
By Road: On A590 Ulverstone Road.
By Rail: Ulverstone.
By Water: Via Windermere Steamers from Bowness & Ambleside for Lakeside Station.
FACILITIES
Shop, Restaurant, Provision For Disabled, Car Parking, Combined Lake/Rail Service.
FARES
Adult return 2.65, Child 1.35, Adult single 1.55, child single 1.02.

Wilson's View
No more cheap laughs about daffodils or what words are worth - let the line speak for itself.
At Haverthwaite, there is a splendid example of a country station, which now has the added
attraction of a venerable old footbridge, once sited on the ECML. At Lakeside, there is a
ferry terminal, and very few railways anywhere can boast connections with a regular
passenger ferry as part of their timetable - a trip on the train, round the lake and back again
in time for tea, which can be taken in the convivial surroundings of Haverthwaite Station's
Buffet/Restaurant.

Launceston Steam Railway

When
Table A

Launceston	Dep	11.10	12.00	12.50	14.00	14.40	15.20	16.00	17.00

Table B

Launceston	Dep	11.20	12.00	12.50	14.00	15.00	16.00	17.00

Trains run to Deer Park non-stop journey time 14 minutes.
Returning trains call at Hunts Crossing on request for Riverside Walk and Picnic Area.

Service Operates:
Good Friday to Easter Monday then Sundays and Tuesdays until Spring Bank Holiday, daily except Saturdays from then until end September, Sundays and Tuesdays in October until 31st.

Table A operates at Easter and during daily running.
Table B is in operation during Sunday/Tuesday running period.

Where
LOCATION
Launceston Steam Railway. The Old Gas Works, St Thomas Road, Launceston PL15 8DA.
Telephone (0566)775665.
ACCESS
By Road: Launceston is on A388.
By Rail: Exeter.
FACILITIES
Shop, Buffet, Museum, Robey Engine, Car & Coach Parking.
FARES
Adults 3.00, Child/O.A.P 1.70, Families 8.90, Dogs 50p, Under 3's free. Discount for parties.
LOCOS
Hunslets No317, Lilian, No679 Covercoat, No409 Velinheli.

Wilson's View
This charming narrow gauge line, which is laid on the trackbed of the former LSWR route from Halwill to Padstow, was once the haunt of such famous trains as the Atlantic Coast Express. Today, the line is no longer the haunt of express trains but, as you chuff sedately along the beautiful Kensey Valley behind one of the line's immaculately restored old Hunslet Quarry engines, you may just hear the distant echo of the ACE's wailing whistle. Excellent coffee in the buffet too!

Leighton Buzzard Railway

NARROW GAUGE

When

						X
Pages Park	Dep	11.00	12.30	13.50	15.10	16.30
Vandyke Road		R	R	R	R	R
Stonehenge Works	Arr	11.25	12.55	14.15	15.35	16.55
Stonehenge Works	Dep	11.35	13.05	14.25	15.45	17.05
Vandyke Road		R	R	R	R	R
Pages Park	Arr	12.00	13.31	14.51	16.11	17.31

Extra trains at busy periods.

Notes:
(X) Does not run Easter Saturday, Wednesdays or Thursdays.
(R)Trains pick up and set down on request.

Service Operates:
Sundays & Bank Holiday Mondays April 5th to October 4th.
Good Friday & Easter Saturday April 17/18th.
Wednesdays & Thursdays August 5th to September 3rd.

What

Teddy Bears Outing	Sunday May 10th
25th Birthday Steam Gala	Sunday June 21st
Steam Festival	Operating days between August 2nd & September 13th
Festival Steam up '92	Saturday & Sunday 12/13th September
Conker Championship	Sunday 4th October
Santa Trains	Dates in December to be announced

Where

LOCATION
Pages's Park Station, Billington Road, Leighton Buzzard, Bedfordshire LU7 8TN.
Telephone (0525) 373888.
ACCESS
By Bus: From Leighton Buzzard B.R. Station.
By Road: Off A5 on A4146 Hemel Hempstead Road.
By Rail: Leighton Buzzard.
FACILITIES
Shop, Buffet, Car Parking, Provision For Disabled, Schools Service, Picnic In Page's Park.
LOCOS
De Winton 0-4-0VBT No1 Chaloner, Orenstein & Koppel 0-6-0WT No5, Elf, Barclay 0-6-0T No4
Doll, Baguley 0-4-0T No3 Rishra, Motor Rail 4WDM No43 & No18 Feanor, Hunslet 0-4-0 Alice,
Orenstein & Koppel 0-4-0WT P C Allen, Kerr Stuart 0-4-0ST Peter Pan.
FARES
Adult return 3.50, O.A.P 2.80 and Children (5-15) 1.75, under 5's free. Family Fare Discounts.

Wilson's View

Parables suggest not building houses on sand. However, this is the sole reason for the existence of the LBR, that's Leighton Buzzard Railway not Lynton & Barnstaple. In railway terms, the line is a young upstart - it opened for traffic in 1919 and, despite its sandy foundations, it has survived and prospered. The line's steam fleet is a very variegated bunch, an 0-4-0VBT de Winton, a Kerr Stuart Wren class 0-4-0ST, a Baguley, a Barclay and a pair of Orenstein & Koppels, one an 0-6-0, the other an 0-4-0. These locos have come from far and wide, from Cornwall to the Cameroon, Spain and even India. LBR - loverly birra railway!

Llanberis Lake Railway

NARROW GAUGE

Rheilfford Llyn Padarn Cyf

When

Table A

Padarn Park   Dep   11.30   13.00   14.00   15.00   (PTOT)
March 2nd to April 9th & October 5th to 29th Monday to Thursday only.

Table B

	SX	SX				NF
Padarn Park Dep	11.00	11.45	13.00	14.00	15.00	16.00

Mondays to Fridays 13th April to May 22nd Sundays May 3rd & May 24th Sunday to Friday May 29th to June 28th Fridays only June 29th to September 11th, Sunday to Friday September 13th to October 2nd also Easter Saturday and Sunday April 18/19th

Table C

	SX	SX								
Padarn Park Dep	11.00	11.45	12.30	13.00	13.30	14.00	14.30	15.00	15.30	16.00	16.30

May 25th to 28th Sunday to Thursday, June 29th to September 11th Sundays to Thursdays.

Table D

Padarn Park   Dep 13.00   14.00   15.00   16.00

Saturday May 23rd, Sundays May 10/17th, Saturdays June 29th to September 11th except September 5th.

Notes:
(N.F.)   Not Fridays except Good Friday
(S.X.)   Sundays Excepted
(PTOT)   Purchase Ticket on Train (Station Buffet & Shop Closed)

Round trip is 40 minutes from Padarn Park to Penllyn.

Where

LOCATION
Gilfach Ddu, Llanberis, Gwynedd LL55 4TY.
Telephone (0286)870549.
ACCESS
By Bus: Gwynedd Services from Bangor via Caernarvon.
By Road: On A 4086 Caernarvon/Betws-y coed Road.
By Rail: Bangor.
FACILITIES
Shop, Buffet, Provision for Disabled, Car & Coach Parking, Museum, (North Wales Quarrying Museum), Nature Trail, Craft Shops, Picnic Site (Ceillydan).
FARES
Adults 3.40, Children 2.00. Family 8.80 2 Adults & 2 Children.

Wilson's View

Slate, lakes, tourism and 0-4-0 Hunslets make the Llanberis Lake. The line is not the original quarry railway, which was of four foot gauge; it is a purpose-built line laid over the original trackbed. The Llanberis Lake Railway, as its name suggests, runs along the shoreline of the lake which bears its name. From the line, one not only has a view of the lake but also of Snowdon and the locos at work on it.

Llangollen Railway

When

Table A

Llangollen Departures at approx. 90 minute intervals commencing at 11.00hrs until 17.00hrs. These services will call at Berwyn & Deeside Halt and Glyndwfrydy. Services to Glyndwfrydy will begin during 1992.

Table B

On Table B dates departures from Llangollen will be approximately at 60 minute intervals On the following dates the services are diesels. February 1/8/22/29, April 6/10/13/27, May 1/8/ 11/15/18/22, June 1/5/8/12/15/19, September 14/18/21/25/28, October 2/5/9/12/16, November 7/14/21.

Services Operate

Table A
Sundays in January, Saturdays and Sundays in February except 15th/16th, daily April 4th to June 27th and September 5th to October 25th with the following exceptions: Sundays March 1st to November 1st, Bank Holiday Mondays, Good Friday, other exceptions are March 21st, April 18th/25th, May 30th, June 13th, June 27th to September 5th, September 19th, October 3rd/31st.

Table B
Sundays March 1st to November 1st. Bank Holidays & special event days including April 17th & 20th, May 4th & 25th & August 31st. This table also applies on February 15th/16th, March 21st, April 18th and 25th, May 30th, June 13th daily from June 27th to September 5th then September 19th, October 3rd & 31st. This table also applies to Santa Services on December 6/ 12/13/19/20th.
At the time of going to press timings had not been agreed because of the planned opening to Glyndwfrydy. However, the dates of operation are correct as are the special events listings.

What

Mince Pie Specials	January 1st-5th 1992.
Thomas Events	February 15/16th, March 21/22nd, April 25/26th, May 30/31st, June 27/28th, September 5/6th, October 3/4th & 31st, November 1st
Steam Gala	June 13/14th
Schools Week	June 29th-July 3rd
Eisteddfod Week	July 8th-12th
Transport Extravaganza	September 19/20th
Santa Trains	November 28/29th, December 5/6/12/13/18th-24th
Mince Pie Specials	December 26th-January 3rd 1993

Berwyn Belle Wine & Dine Services Run On:
January 25/26th, February 29th, March 1st & 28th/29th, April 25/26th, May 16/17th, 23/24th, June 13/14/27/28th, July 10/11/12 then weekly until 12/13th September, September 26/27th, October 24/25th, November 28/29th, December 19/20th.

The Saturday dates are an evening service and the Sunday dates are a Sunday Luncheon service.

Where

LOCATION

Llangollen Station, Abbey Road, Llangollen, Clwyd LL20 8SN.

Telephone (0978)860951 (Talking Timetable) (0978) 860979 Bookings/Enquiries.

ACCESS

By Bus: From Ruabon Crosville Services to Llangollen.

By Road: On A542 off A5 between Chirk & Corwen.

By Rail: Ruabon.

FACILITIES

Shop, Buffet, Provision for Disabled, Car Parking (Town Centre), Signal Box Access, Wine & Dine Service (Booking Essential).

LOCOS

Ex-LMS 0-6-0T 7298, Ex-GWR 4-6-0 7822 Foxcote Manor, 0-6-0ST Burtonwood Brewer, 0-6-0ST Darfield No1. Visiting locos Ex-GWR 2-6-2T 4566, Ex-LNER 0-6-0 2392.

Wilson's View

The Glyndwfrydy extension should open this year, as the Llangollen rolls towards its goal of Corwen by 1996. Llangollen Station itself must rank as one of the most unique in the country - if you step over the edge of platform two, you'll fall in the Dee. Another very attractive feature at Llangollen is the well-kept, wild flower gardens which decorate the platforms. The unmistakable whiff of the Great Way Round hovers over the proceedings - chocolate and cream stock and a Manor to Hall (sic) them. There's even a secret ingredient - project X.

Lochty Private Railway

STANDARD GAUGE

When

Departures are approximately every 30 minutes from 13.45 to 17.00

Service Operate:

Sundays June 7th to September 6th

Where

LOCATION

Lochty Farm, nr Arncroach, Fife.

Postal Contact: C/O 23 Millfield, Cupar, Fife, Scotland KY15 5UT.

ACCESS

By Bus: Fife Scottish Service 95 (Leven-Dundee), as far as Crail then 7 mile walk or taxi.

By Road: Cupar - Crail Road B940 7 miles from Crail, the A915 or A917 link with B940.

By Rail: Cupar, Markinch, Leuchars.

FACILITIES

Shop/Visitor Centre, Provision For Disabled, Car & Coach Parking. 10% Discount On Parties of Ten or More.

Wilson's View

This line is the private fief of one J.B.Cameron, Chairman of Scot Rail and owner of No9, a.k.a. Osprey, Union of South Africa, and Merlin! However, No.9 does not live at Lochty, but another of Sir Nigel's products does - an observation saloon. Motive power at Lochty is provided by the likes of Peckett, Bagnall or Barclay. Another of the Lochty's claims to fame is that it was the first standard gauge preserved railway in Scotland.

Mangapps Farm Museum

STANDARD GAUGE

When

13.00 to 18.00
Saturdays, Sundays & Bank Holidays except Christmas (all year). Every Wednesday Easter to the end of September. Daily in July & August.

Unlimited rides on all public open days with steam haulage on Bank Holidays and at least one Sunday per month during the Summer Season. (Phone for steam details.)

Where

LOCATION
Mangapps Farm Railway Museum, Southminster Road, Burnham-On-Crouch, Essex CMO 8QQ.
Telephone (0621) 784898.
ACCESS
By Bus: Eastern National/Hedingham Omnibus passes entrance.
By Road: On B1021 1 mile north of Burnham-On-Crouch.
By Rail: Burnham-On-Crouch (1 mile).
FACILITIES
Shop, Buffet, Car & Coach Parking, Extensive Museum, Parties Anytime By Prior Appointment.
LOCOS
Ex-N.C.B. 0-6-0ST Demelza, Ex-B.R. D2325, 03 399, D8233, Ex-C.E.G.B. Elland No 1.

Wilson's View

Created from a greenfield site by the enthusiasm of its operator, Mr John Jolly, this museum and demonstration line has some fine displays of small exhibits and a collection of wagons, some of Victorian vintage. There are also relics here from the mid-Suffolk railway and a redundant barn which has been turned into an exhibition hall. The motive power is ex-NCB 0-6-0ST Demelza.

The Battlefield Line

STANDARD GAUGE

Market Bosworth Light Railway

When

Shackerstone	Dep	11.00	12.30	13.50	14.00	15.10	16.00	16.30
Mkt.Bosworth	Arr	11.14	12.44	14.04	14.24	15.24	16.14	16.44
Mkt.Bosworth	Dep	11.15	12.45	14.05	14.25	15.25	16.15	16.45
Shenton	Arr	11.25	12.55	14.15	14.35	15.35	16.25	16.55
Shenton	Dep	11.35	13.05	14.25	14.45	15.45	16.40	17.05
Mkt.Bosworth	Arr	11.43	13.13	14.33	14.55	15.53	16.45	17.13
Mkt.Bosworth	Dep	11.44	13.14	14.34	14.56	15.54	16.46	17.14
Shackerstone	Arr	12.00	13.30	14.40	15.10	16.10	17.00	17.30

Notes: A runs Sundays during October only. B runs 15 minutes later on August 23rd.

Service Operate:
Easter and every Sunday & Bank Holiday until the end of October.
The site is open every weekend, (not Saturdays Jan-Mar), throughout the year 11.30 to 17.30.

What

The Shenton extension will be subject to Railway Inspectorate approval, open in April. There will be numerous special events during the year, see press for details.

Where

LOCATION
Shackerstone Station, Nr Market Bosworth, Leicestershire.
ACCESS
By Bus: From Leicester Market Bosworth Service.
By Road: On B585 off A444 Burton-On-Trent Nuneaton Road.
By Rail: Hinckley or Nuneaton.
FACILITIES
Shop, Buffet, Car & Coach Parking (Shackerstone Only), Museum, Coach for Disabled (14 Days Notice).
FARES
Platform Tickets 50p Adults, Children/O.A.P. Free. Train Fares: Adult Return 4.00 Children/O.A.P. 2.00, Family 11.00, Supplement for riding in the observation saloon.

Wilson's View

The extension to- is there a horse in the field? Dick needs it - Shenton might be open just before the end of this season at the Old Vic. Subject, of course, to the approval of the Railway Inspectorate. Slowly but surely the battle is being won - shame Dick won't be around to see it. Wonder if they'll be serving Malmesbury Wine? Whatever the answers they'll be serving them all with steam. A real time machine this line taking one back through the age of steam to the time when Kings ruled and Princes went to Blackpool!

Middleton Railway

When

Saturdays April 18th until 26th September.

Moor Road	Dep	13.30	14.15	15.00	15.45	16.30
Middleton	Arr	13.42	14.27	15.12	15.57	16.42
Middleton	Dep	13.47	14.32	15.17	16.02	16.47
Moor Road	Arr	13.55	14.40	15.25	16.10	16.55

Sundays April 19th until 27th September.

Moor Road	Dep	13.00	13.30	14.00	14.30	15.00	15.30	16.00	16.30
Middleton	Arr	13.08	13.38	14.08	14.38	15.08	15.38	16.08	16.38
Middleton	Dep	13.13	13.43	14.13	14.43	15.13	15.43	16.13	16.43
Moor Road	Arr	13.20	13.50	14.20	14.50	15.20	15.50	16.20	16.50

Wednesdays.January 1st 1992 & during August only (times also apply to School Day Service).

Moor Road	Dep	13.30	14.15	15.00	15.45	16.30
Middleton	Arr	13.38	14.23	15.08	15.53	16.38
Middleton	Dep	13.43	14.28	15.13	15.58	16.43
Moor Road	Arr	13.50	14.35	15.20	16.05	16.50

Saturday Services normally Diesel.Sundays normally steam haulage.

What

New Year Service	January 1st 1992
Easter Trains	April 18th to 21st
Mayday Trains	May 2nd to 4th
School Trains	May 13th
Spring Bank Holiday	May 23rd to 25th
Friends of Thomas Day	June 27th/28th
60 Years of the Diesel	July 18th
Cops `N' Robbers Day	August 2nd
Bank Holiday Trains	August 29th to 31st
Children's Weekend	September 26th/27th
Santa Trains	December 5/6/12/13/19/20th

Where

LOCATION
The Station, Moor Road, Leeds LS10 2JD.
Telephone (0532)710320/711089 after 6.00pm.
ACCESS
By Bus: Yorkshire Rider Services CB2, 76 or 77.
By Road: Adjacent to exit 45 on M1, the motorway crosses the line just 100yds south of Moor Road Station.
By Rail: Leeds.
FACILITIES
Shop, Buffet, Picnic Area (Middleton Park), Car & Coach Parking, Special Trains and Parties Catered For By Arrangement.
LOCOS
Ex-LNER Sentinel Y1 No54, Ex-Danish Railways 0-4-0WT, No385, 0-4-0ST, Mirvale, Ex-LMS Diesel 7401, Diesels Carol, Mary, 132C (Thos Hill), Brush 91.
FARES
Adults 1.20, Children 60p, special fares apply on Friends of Thomas Day and on Santa Trains.

Wilson's View

Not the longest or the largest line in preservation, though it was the first standard gauge line to be operated by volunteers. Middleton enjoys two other firsts - first railway to be opened under an Act of Parliament in 1758, and the first to make commercial use of steam in 1812. The present day Middleton Railway is the custodian of Leeds' long tradition of locomotive building, and the society's aim is to have a working example of each of the Leeds locomotive builders' products. Like their big brother BR, they're getting there.

Mid-Hants Railway

STANDARD GAUGE

When

Table A

Alresford	Dep	10.30	12.10	**A** 13.55	**B** 14.10	**A** 15.40	**B** 16.00
Ropley	Dep	10.40	12.25	14.11	14.25	15.51	16.11
Medstead	Dep	10.57	12.37	14.23	14.37	16.02	16.22
Alton	Arr	11.03	12.49	14.35	14.49	16.14	16.34

Alton	Dep	11.15	13.05	13.15	**A** 14.55	**B** 15.15	**A** 16.25	**B** 16.45
Medstead	Dep	11.30	13.20	13.30	15.10	15.30	16.40	16.59
Ropley	Dep	11.41	13.31	13.41	15.21	15.41	16.51	17.09
Alresford	Arr	11.49	13.39	13.49	15.29	15.49	16.59	17.17

Table B

Alresford	Dep	10.40	11.15	**X** 12.25	13.05	**Y** 14.15	15.05	**Z** 16.15
Ropley	Dep	10.57	11.30	12.45	13.20	14.40	15.20	16.40
Medstead	Dep	11.08	11.47	12.51	13.42	14.51	15.42	16.51
Alton	Arr	11.20	11.59	13.03	13.54	15.03	15.54	17.03

Alton	Dep	10.30	11.30	**P** 12.15	13.20	**P** 14.15	**Q** 15.20	**P** 16.10	**R** 17.16
Medstead	Dep	10.45	11.45	12.30	13.25	14.30	15.35	16.25	17.31
Ropley	Dep	10.56	11.56	12.42	13.52	14.42	15.52	16.38	17.41
Alresford	Arr	11.04	12.04	12.50	14.00	14.50	16.00	16.46	17.49

Table C

Alresford	Dep	10.40	11.30	12.18	12.35	13.15	13.55	14.35	15.15	15.55	16.35	17.15
Ropley	Dep	10.55	11.53	12.28	13.00	13.40	14.20	15.00	15.40	16.20	17.00	17.35
Medstead	Dep	11.06	12.04	12.41	13.21	14.01	14.41	15.21	16.01	16.41	17.19	17.55
Alton	Arr	11.18	12.16	12.53	13.33	14.13	14.53	15.33	16.13	16.53	17.34	18.07

Alton	Dep	10.30	11.28	12.26	13.05	13.45	14.25	15.05	15.45	16.25	17.03	17.40
Medstead	Dep	10.44	11.43	12.41	13.20	14.00	14.40	15.20	16.00	16.40	17.17	17.54
Ropley	Dep	10.56	11.56	12.52	13.31	14.11	14.51	15.31	16.11	16.51	17.27	18.04
Alresford	Arr	11.04	12.04	13.00	13.39	14.19	14.59	15.39	16.19	16.59	17.35	18.12

Notes: A runs Sundays only in January/February & March, B runs after February 26th, but not Sundays in March.

X arrives 8 mins later, Y 13 mins later and Z 3 mins later on April 12/19/26th, May 3/10/17/25/31st, June 14/21st, July 12/26th, August 2/9/16/30/31st, September 13/20/27th, October 4th & November 1st.

P departs 5 mins earlier & Q 6 mins later on the dates as above & R only runs on those dates.

Services Operate:

Table A: Sundays January 5th to March 22nd, Wednesday & Thursday February 26/27th, Monday March 23rd, May 26th to 29th, Tuesday to Thursday June 2nd to July 23rd, September 1st to 4th, October 10/17/24/31st, May 28th to 31st, Tuesday to Thursday June 4th to July 18th, July 22nd to 26th, September 2nd to 6th, October 12th/23rd/26th.

Table B: April 11/12/17th to 20th/25/26th, May 2nd to 4th/9/10/16/17/23rd to 25th/30/31st, June 14/20/21st, July 4/11/12/18th, daily July 25th to August 31st except August 23rd, September 5/12/13/19/20/26/27th, October 3/4/11/25th.

Table C: April 4/5th, May 24th, June 6/7th/27/28th, July 5th/19th, August 23rd, September 6th, October 18th.

What

New for 1992 the Countryman. This service is dedicated to catering and will carry only people who have booked. It will depart Alresford at 11.40 & 15.45 and from Alton at 12.45. The operational dates are as follows: April 12/19/26th, May 3/10/17/25/31st, June 14/21st, July 12/26th, August 2/9/16/30/31st, September 13/20/27th, October 4th & November 1st.

Table C dates are those on which special events are being held and the most intensive services are operated.

Santa Trains   November 28/29th/December 5/6/12/13/19th to 24th
Mince Pie Service December 26th to January 1st.

Where

LOCATION
Alresford Station, Alresford, Hants SO24 9JG.
Telephone (096273) 3810.
ACCESS
By Bus: From Winchester Alder Valley Service to Alresford.
By Road: Off A31 Winchester/Alton Road.
By Rail: Winchester or Alton. The line shares Alton Station with B.R.
FACILITIES
Shop, Buffet, Picnic Area (Ropley). Wine & Dine Pullman, Children's Birthday Party Service, Provision for Disabled, Car & Coach Parking, Museum.
LOCOS
Ex-SR. 4-6-2 34105 Swanage, Ex-SR 2-6-0 31806, 31874, 31625, Ex-LSWR 4-6-0 506, Ex-BR. 2-6-0 76017, Ex-LMR No 601 Sturdee, Ex-USATC Baldwin 2-8-0.
FARES
Adults 4.65 (Unlimited Travel), Children 3.00, Pensioners 3.50, Family 2 Adults and up to 4 Children 12.95, Party Concessions on 20 +, Single Fares available.
These are the 1991 prices, rates for 1992 not advised.

Wilson's View

Not only is the Mid-Hants one of Britain's leading lines, it is also one of the most heavily graded - it wasn't known as `The Alps' for nothing. Opened as the Alton and Winchester Railway it became part of the LSWR and, subsequently, the Southern. The present day railway still has that unmistakable SR feel about it, and the loco fleet goes a long way towards creating that image. Rebuilt and un-rebuilt Bulleid Pacifics, Urie's S15 and Maunsell's Moguls provide a fine fleet of Southern steam. The Southern flavour is further enhanced by the stations and signalling.

Ex-GWR Castle class 4-6-0 5029 Nunney Castle gets away from Loughborough Central on one of her running-in turns.

Midland Railway Centre

NARROW GAUGE MINIMUM GAUGE STANDARD GAUGE

When
Winter Service

			A			C
Butterley	Dep	11.30	12.45	13.59	15.05	16.15
Swanwick Jct	Arr	11.34	12.49	14.00	15.09	16.19
Swanwick Jct	Dep	11.36	12.51	14.02	15.11	16.21
Ironville	Arr	11.42	12.57	14.07	15.17	16.27
Ironville	Dep	11.52	13.07	14.17	15.27	16.37
Swanwick Jct	Arr	11.58	13.13	14.23	15.33	16.43
Swanwick Jct	Dep	12.04	13.19	14.29	15.39	17.03
Butterley	Passes Straight Through					
Hammersmith	Arr	12.09	13.24	14.34	15.44	17.08
Hammersmith	Dep	12.19	13.34	14.44	15.54	17.18
Butterley	Arr	12.21	13.36	14.46	15.56	17.20

High Season Service

				A		C
Butterley	Dep	11.15	12.30	14.00	15.00	16.15
Swanwick Jct	Arr	11.19	12.34	14.04	15.04	16.19
Swanwick Jct	Dep	11.21	12.36	14.06	15.06	16.21
Riddings	Arr	11.27	12.42	14.12	15.12	16.27
Riddings	Dep	11.37	12.52	14.22	15.22	16.37
Swanwick Jct	Arr	11.43	12.58	14.28	15.28	16.43
Swanwick Jct	Dep	11.49	13.04	14.34	15.34	17.03
Butterley	Passes Straight Through					
Hammersmith	Arr	11.54	13.09	14.39	15.39	17.08
Hammersmith	Dep	12.04	13.19	14.49	15.49	17.18
Butterley	Arr	12.06	13.21	14.51	15.51	17.20

Two Train Service

				A						B
Butterley	Dep	11.15	12.10	12.45	13.20	13.55	14.30	15.05	15.40	16.15
Swanwick Jct	Arr	11.19	12.14							
Swanwick Jct	Dep	11.21	12.16							
Riddings	Arr	11.27	12.22	12.57	13.32	14.07	14.42	15.17	15.52	16.27
Riddings	Dep	11.37	12.32	13.07	13.42	14.17	14.52	15.27	16.02	16.37
Swanwick Jct	Arr	11.43	12.38	13.13	13.48	14.23	14.58	15.33	16.08	16.43
Swanwick Jct	Dep	11.49	12.45	13.20	13.55	14.30	15.05	15.40	16.15	17.03
Butterley	Passes Straight Through									
Hammersmith	Arr	11.54	12.55	13.30	14.05	14.40	15.15	15.50	16.25	17.08
Hammersmith	Dep	12.04	13.05	13.40	14.15	14.50	15.25	16.00	16.35	17.18
Butterley	Arr	12.06	13.07	13.42	14.17	14.52	15.27	16.02	16.37	17.20

Notes: Winter Service - (A) Midlander Sunday Lunch Train
(C) Does not operate January or 2nd/9th February
Two Train Service: (B) Afternoon tea served on this service. (A) Sunday Lunch Train.

Narrow gauge trains run from Butterley Park to Brands Sidings on Sundays and Bank Holiday Mondays April to September 12.00 to 17.00 as required. Miniature trains (3 1/2" to 5" gauge) Sundays and Bank Holiday Mondays, Easter to the end of September from 13.00 to 17.00.

Winter Service Dates
January   5/12/19/26th   February 2/9/16/23rd
March   7/15/22/28th   November 7/8/15/22nd

Mid Season Service Dates
April   4/11/17/18/21st-25th
May   2/9/16/26th-30th
June   3/6/10/13/17/20/24/27/30th
July   1st-4th/7th-11th/14th-16th/21st-24th/28th-31st

August	1st/3rd-8th/10th-15th/17th-22nd/25th-29th
September	1st-4th/9/12/16/19/26th
October	3/10/24/26th-November 1st

Two Train Service Dates
March	8/29th
April	5/12/19/20/26th
May	3/4/10/17/23rd-25th/31st
June	7/14/21/28th
July	5/12/18/19/25/26th
August	2/9/16/23/24/30/31st
September	5/6/13/20/27th
October	4/11/17/18/25th

School Service Dates:
Wednesdays: April 8/15/29th. May 13th/20th. September 23/30th. October 7/14/21st.
School Services are also available on High Season Wednesdays between May & September.

Mid-Day Midlander
Sunday Luncheon Trains Service Dates: Every Sunday except May 25th until November 22nd.

What

Thomas Events	March 7/8th, May 23rd-31st, August 8th-16th, October 24-Nov 1st
Mother's Day Event	March 29th (Special Lunch Service)
Railway Art Show	April 18th-20th & August 29-31st
Road Transport Display	May 10th & September 13th
Diesel/Steam Weekend	April 4/5th, May 16/17th, June 20/21st, August 22/23rd, Sept 19/20th
Easter Steaming	April 17th-26th
May Day Steaming	May 2nd-4th
Father's Day Event	June 21st
Toy Town Weekend	June 27/28th & September 12/13th. Free to kids with Teddy
Country Park Event	July 4/5th
Road Transport Rally	July 12th
Summer Steam Gala	July 25/26th
Night Steam Event	August 1st
Austin 7 Rally	August 2nd
Miniature Railway Gala	30/31st
Disabled Weekend	August 1/2nd. Free to registered disabled.
Vintage Weekend	September 5/6th
Narrow Gauge Event	September 26/27th
Autumn Diesel Gala	October 17/18th
Bonfire Night Event	November 7th
Santa Service	November 28/29th, December 5/6/12/13/19th to 24th
Boxing Day /Mince Pie Spl.	December 26th-31st
New Year Trains	January 1st 1993

Where

LOCATION
Butterley Station, Nr Ripley, Derbyshire.
Telephone (0773) 74674/749788 or 570140.
ACCESS
By Bus: From Derby or Alfreton Trent Services.
By Road: On A61 just north of Ripley (signposted from A38).
By Rail: Derby or Alfreton.
FACILITIES
Shop, Buffet, Museum, Picnic & Children's Play Area, Sunday Lunch Trains, Evening Charter
Trains (Minimum 40 People), Joint Booking with Tramway Museum at Crich, Car & Coach
Parking, 35 Acre Country Park.

FARES
Adults 3.50, Child 1.75, O.A.P. 3.00, Family 8.75.
Sundays April to September Adults 4.00, Child 2.00 O.A.P. 3.00, Family 10.00.
LOCOS
Ex-LMS 4-6-2 Princess Margaret Rose, Ex-LMS 4-6-0 44932.
Ex-S&DJR 2-8-0 7F 53809, Ex-B.R. 9F 92214, Ex-LMS 0-6-0T 47564.
Ex-BR 2-6-4T 80080, Diesel D4 Great Gable, 55-015 Tulyar, 40-012 Aureol 45-133 Locos and
rolling stock exhibited in museum, Ex-MR 2-4-0 158A, Ex-LNWR 0-8-0 9395, 0-4-0ST Gladys,
0-4-0F, Ex MR Royal Saloon, T.P.O. L&Y Family Saloon, MR Six Wheel Brake 3RD, MR Brake
Van.

Wilson's View

A fine museum and workshops are complemented by an amazing diversity of exhibits,
activities and gauges. There are all sizes of trains in operation at the MRC from O gauge
garden railways through minimum and narrow gauges, to four feet eight and a half inch
gauge. The motive power is as catholic as the gauges, diminutive Jinties to one of Stanier's
first Pacifics, a 2-8-0 from the S&D plus the inevitable Black 5. MRC also has a selection of
ex-mainline diesel locomotives which see service on the weekends, when mixed traction is
used.

Moors Valley Railway

MINIMUM GAUGE

When
Every Saturday and Sunday, daily from one week before to one week after Easter and Spring Bank Holiday to mid September, also during school half terms and from December 27th to the end of the school holidays.
Opening times 10.45 to 17.00

What
Special events throughout the year, see local press for details.
Sundays double - reverse run at 12.00hrs.

Where
LOCATION
Moors Valley Country Park, Horton Road, Ashley Heath, Nr.Ringwood, Hants BH24 2ET
Telephone: (0425) 471415
ACCESS
By Bus: Service from Bournemouth (infrequent)
By Road: Horton Road is just off the A31 at the junction between the A31 & the A338
By Rail: Bournemouth/Christchurch
FACILITIES
Buffet, Adventure Playground, Picnic Area, Shop, Car & Coach Parking, 9 Hole Golf Course and Driving Range, Forest Walks.
LOCOS
0-4-2T No.3 Talos, 0-4-2T No.4 Tinkerbell, 4-6-0 No.5 Sapper, 2-6-2T No.6 Medea, 2-6-4T No.7 Aelfred, 2-4-4T No.9 Jason, 2-6-2 No.10 Offa, 2-6-2 No.11 Zeus, 2-4-0TT No.12 Petra.

Wilson's View
One of the new entries for the 1992 edition, this seven and a quarter inch gauge system has much to recommend it. There's a classic loco shed and turntable, full semaphore signalling, tunnels, bridges and an elegant terminal station. The railway run freight as well as passenger services and they even have a Wall's Ice Cream Freight van - not a bad effort when you consider the gauge this line is laid to.

National Railway Museum

STANDARD GAUGE

When

Monday to Saturday 10.00 to 18.00. Sundays 11.00 to 18.00.
Daily except Christmas Eve, Christmas Day, New Year's Day & Boxing Day.

What

` The Great Railway Show', many previously undisplayed items will be 'on show'. These displays
will be in the former York Goods Station, which is the Museum's new venue whilst repairs are
made to the roof of the main exhibition hall. The theme for the new show will be travelling by
train for both goods and passengers.

The newly refurbished main exhibition hall will re-open on Wednesday April 15th with new
displays and exhibits detailing the story of the railways up to the present day.

Where

LOCATION
The National Railway Museum, Leeman Road, York YO2 4XJ. Telephone (0904)621261.
ACCESS
By Bus: National Bus Services from most towns to York.
By Road: Via A1/A59 from North, A1/A64 from South.
By Rail: York (5 minutes walk).
FACILITIES
Shop, Buffet/Restaurant, Model Railway, Picture Gallery, Education Service, Provision for
Disabled, Mother & Baby Room, Reference Libary (Apply For Readers Ticket), Car Parking.
The Museum Is available for private viewings and conferences by contacting:
The Marketing Officer (Mr.C. O. Wardroper).

Wilson's View

**This venerable institution is more than just a museum, it forms part of the national archive,
with thousands of books, records and photographs in addition to the more obvious examples
of railway history, locos and rolling stock. The museum provides drawings and diagrams
from which preservationists can recreate or fabricate anything from a footbridge to a
footplate. The museum also maintains and operates, on the mainline, a number of famous
locomotives. All in all there is a great deal more to the NRM than meets the eye.**

*Ex-SR Schools class 4-4-0 30926 Repton passes the mailcatcher just south of Quorn & Woodhouse, on
the Great Central Railway.*

THE FULL PICTURE!

When

Table A

Wansford	Dep	11.30	13.15	15.00	16.30
Yarwell	Arr	11.35	13.20	15.05	16.35
Yarwell	Dep	11.41	13.26	15.11	16.41
Wansford		11.50	13.35	15.20	16.45
Ferry Meadow		12.03	13.48	15.33	16.58
Orton Mere		12.09	13.54	15.39	17.04
Peterborough	Arr	12.15	14.00	15.45	17.10
Peterborough	Dep	12.30	14.15	16.00	17.15
Orton Mere		12.37	14.23	16.07	17.22
Ferry Meadow		12.42	14.28	16.12	17.27
Wansford	Arr	12.55	14.40	16.25	17.39

Table D

Wansford	Dep	11.00	12.30	14.00
Yarwell	Arr	11.05	12.35	14.05
Yarwell	Dep	11.11	12.41	14.11
Wansford		11.15	12.45	14.15
Ferry Meadow		11.28	12.58	14.28
Orton Mere		11.34	13.04	14.34
Peterborough	Arr	11.40	13.10	14.40
Peterborough	Dep	11.50	13.20	14.50
Orton Mere		11.57	13.27	14.57
Ferry Meadow		12.02	13.32	15.02
Wansford	Arr	12.14	13.44	15.14

Table B

Wansford	Dep	10.30	12.00	13.30	15.00	16.30
Yarwell	Arr	10.35	12.05	13.35	15.05	16.35
Yarwell	Dep	10.41	12.11	13.41	15.11	16.41
Wansford		10.45	12.15	13.45	15.15	16.45
Ferry Meadow		10.58	12.28	13.58	15.28	16.58
Orton Mere		11.04	12.34	14.04	15.34	17.04
Peterborough	Arr	11.10	12.40	14.10	15.40	17.10
Peterborough	Dep	11.20	12.50	14.20	15.50	17.20
Orton Mere		11.27	12.57	14.27	15.57	17.27
Ferry Meadow		11.32	13.02	14.32	16.02	17.32
Wansford	Arr	11.44	13.14	14.44	16.14	17.44

Table C

		BMO						
Wansford	Dep	10.30	11.30	12.30	13.30	14.30	15.30	16.30
Yarwell	Arr	10.35	11.35	12.35	13.35	14.35	15.35	16.35
Yarwell	Dep	10.41	11.41	12.41	13.41	14.41	15.41	16.41
Wansford		10.45						16.55
Ferry Meadow		10.58	11.58	12.58	13.58	14.58	15.58	17.08
Orton Mere		11.04	12.04	13.04	14.04	15.04	16.04	17.14
Peterborough	Arr	11.10	12.10	13.10	14.10	15.10	16.10	17.20
Peterborough	Dep	11.20	12.20	13.20	14.20	15.20	16.20	17.30
Orton Mere		11.27	12.27	13.27	14.27	15.27	16.27	17.35
Ferry Meadow		11.32	12.32	13.32	14.32	15.32	16.32	17.40
Wansford	Arr	11.44	12.44	13.44	14.44	15.44	16.44	17.52

Trains do not pick up at Wansford on return from Yarwell, except the 10.00 & 17.00 departures, which stop to pick up at Wansford at 10.16 & 17.20.

Service Operates
Table A: Saturdays April to October, February 29th, March 7th and Good Friday April 17th.
Sundays March, April, May, September and October. Weekdays mid-July to end of August.
Table B: Sundays in June, July and August.
Table C: Bank Holiday Saturday, Sunday and Monday plus all major events.
Table D: February 23, 26 and 27th, weekdays mid-June to mid-July, Sundays in November.
Notes: Table C (BMO) Bank Holiday Monday only.

What

School Specials	February 23, 26 and 27th.
Britannia's Spring Outing	February 29th, March 1st.
Enthusiasts Weekend	March 7, 8th.
Mothers Day Special	March 29th.
Friends of Thomas Weekend	April 4, 5th.
Easter Egg Specials	April 17-20th.
Bank Holiday Steam Weekends	May 2-4th, 23-25th.
Teddy Bears Weekend	June 6-7th.
Fathers Day Specials	June 21st.
Thomas's 21st Birthday	June 26-28th.
Vintage Weekend	July 11, 12th.
Meet the Driver	July 24, 25th.
Diesel Gala	August 1, 2nd.
Thomas's Big Weekend	August 15, 16th.
Bank Holiday Steam	August 29-31st.
Enthusiasts Weekend	September 12, 13th.
Photographic Weekend	October 10th.
Autumn Schools Out	October 21, 24, 25, 28 and 29th.
Halloween	October 31st.
Firework Fiesta	November 7th (provisional).
Santa Specials	December (dates to be announced)

Where

LOCATION
Wansford Station, Old North Road, Stibbington, Peterborough PE8 6LR. Telephone (0780)782854.
ACCESS
By Bus: From Peterborough, services to Orton Mere or Ferry Meadow.
By Road: Beside A1 at Stibbington.
By Rail: Peterborough.
FACILITIES
Shop, Buffet, Provision for Disabled, Wagon Lits Restaurant Coach
(advance booking essential), Schools Service,
Car & Coach Parking, Museum.
LOCOS
Ex-LMS 4-6-0 5231, Ex-Swedish Railways 2-6-2T 1178,
Austerity 0-6-0T 68081, 0-6-0T 1800 Thomas,
Diesels D9516, 14029 and visiting locos.

Wilson's View

This line from Wansford to Peterborough was once a part of the London & North Western's empire, though today it has a very cosmopolitan image with locomotives from Continental Europe as well as those of a more home-spun nature. The diverse motive power fleet is complemented by equally diverse rolling stock, and this combination of British and Continental designs has helped the NVR to gain much valuable work as a film location. This year, the line could well be enjoying the benefits of the return to steam of un-rebuilt B-o-B 34081 92 Squadron.

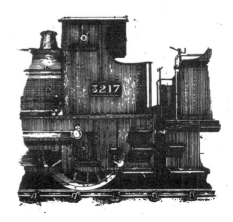

North Downs Steam Railway

When
Every Sunday from February 2nd throughout the year. Saturdays from June to September inclusive.
Trains run at regular intervals between 11.00 and 17.00 or dusk.

What
Santa Trains run November 29th and December 6,12,13,19 and 20th.

Where
LOCATION
North Downs Steam Railway, Stone Lodge Centre, Cotton Lane, Stone, Nr Dartford, Kent. Telephone (0322) 28260.
ACCESS
By Bus: From Dartford, Kentish Bus 480/481 to Stone Lodge Farm.
By Road: M25 Jct 1a, follow Stone Lodge and Historic Dartford signs.
By Rail: Dartford.
FACILITIES
Shop, Buffet, Car & Coach parking.
LOCOS
RSH 0-6-0T 7846, Bagnall 0-6-0T Topham. There is also a large collection of operational industrial diesel traction.
FARES
Adults 1.20, Children and OAP 60p.

Wilson's View
The NDSR is part of the growing Stone Lodge leisure complex, located close to the Southern end of the Dartford Tunnel. The view from the line is of the Thames, and one can see the new bridge built to carry the motorway across the river in addition to a collection of Ex-Industrial Steam and Diesel locomotives. The whole of the NDSR has been created on a greenfield site after the society's original plans to use part of the trackbed between Fawkham Junction and Southfleet had to be abandoned.

North Norfolk Railway

When
Table A

			P			D
Sheringham	Dep	11.00	12.30	14.00	15.30	17.00
Weybourne	Arr	11.12	12.42	14.12	15.42	17.08
Weybourne	Dep	11.15	12.44	14.14	15.44	17.10
Kelling	Dep	A	A	A	A	17.13
Holt	Arr	11.24	12.57	14.27	15.57	17.20
Holt	Dep	11.35	13.05	14.35	16.05	17.19
Kelling	Dep	R	R	R	R	17.24
Weybourne	Arr	11.44	13.14	14.44	16.14	17.26
Weybourne	Dep	12.00	13.30	15.00	16.30	17.27
Sheringham	Arr	12.13	13.42	15.12	16.42	17.35

Table B: Diesel Railbus Service

Sheringham	Dep	09.45	12.30	14.00	15.30	17.00
Weybourne	Arr	09.53	12.38	14.08	15.38	17.08
Weybourne	Dep	09.54	12.39	14.09	15.39	17.09
Kelling	Dep	09.56	12.41	14.11	15.41	17.11
Holt	Arr	10.02	12.47	14.17	15.47	17.17

Holt	Dep	10.05	12.50	14.20	15.50	17.18
Kelling	Dep	10.10	12.55	14.25	15.55	17.23
Weybourne	Arr	10.12	12.57	14.27	15.57	17.25
Weybourne	Dep	10.15	13.00	14.40	16.00	17.26
Sheringham	Arr	10.24	13.09	14.53	16.09	17.35

Table C

		D			WSOP		WSO		D
Sheringham	Dep	10.00	11.00	12.30	13.15	14.00	14.45	15.30	17.00
Weybourne	Arr	10.08	11.12	12.42	13.27	14.12	14.57	15.42	17.08
Weybourne	Dep	10.09	11.15	12.45	13.30	14.15	15.00	15.45	17.09
Kelling	Dep	10.11	A	A	A	A	A	A	17.11
Holt	Arr	10.17	11.24	12.54	13.39	14.24	15.09	15.54	17.17
		D			WSO		WSO		D
Holt	Dep	10.20	11.35	13.05	13.50	14.35	15.20	16.05	17.20
Kelling	Dep	10.25	R	R	R	R	R	R	17.25
Weybourne	Arr	10.27	11.44	13.14	13.59	14.44	15.29	16.14	17.27
Weybourne	Dep	10.30	12.00	13.30	14.15	15.00	15.45	16.30	17.30
Sheringham	Arr	10.38	12.12	13.42	14.27	15.12	15.57	16.42	17.38

Notes: (D) Diesel traction (WSO) Sunday & Wednesday only (R) Request (A) Does not stop (P) Pullman Diner Train. Minor changes in times may be needed if the BR services to Sheringham alter significantly in 1992.

Service Operates:
Table A: April 5th. Sundays & Wednesdays in April and May. Daily (except Mondays) June to July 19th and from September 6th to end of October.
Table B: Saturdays in May and October. Friday & Saturday in June to July 13th and through September.
Table C: Daily July 18th to September 6th.
Additional services run on Sundays in March and November departing Sheringham at 12.30, 14.30 and 15.30.

What

Thomas Events	April 18-20th, October 24-26th.
Gala Weekend	Early June, exact dates undecided, see press (return of B12).
Rail Trail	June 7th, sponsored walk and ride for charity.
Santa Trains	December 5,6,12,13,19th to 23rd.
Mince Pie Trains	December 27-31st.

Where

LOCATION
The Station, Sheringham, Norfolk NR26 8RA. Telephone (0263)822045.
ACCESS
By Bus: Adjacent to Sheringham Bus Station.
By Road: On A149 Cromer/Wells Road.
By Rail: Sheringham 300 yds (through booking).
FACILITIES
Shop, Buffet, Museum, Car & Coach Parking, Lunch Trains, Nature Trail.

Wilson's View

Running through splendid coastal scenery from the resort town of Sheringham to the village of Holt, the NNR is based on what was once part of the Midland and Great Northern Joint Railway. Indeed, the society which opened and operates the line is the Midland & Great Northern Joint Railway Preservation Society - even more of a mouthful than Wilson's Preserved Steam Railway Timetable. At Weybourne there is a beautiful country station and the railway's purpose-built workshops.
In the not-too-distant future, the North Norfolk will be the proud operators of the only surviving inside-cylinder 4-6-0 in the country - the ex-LNER B12 61572.

North Staffordshire Railway

STANDARD GAUGE

When
11.00 to 17.30. Sundays & Bank Holiday Mondays, Easter to September.
Steam Days: April 19, 20th. May 3, 4, 10, 24 and 25th. June 7th. July 13th. August 2, 9, 16, 25, 30 and 31st. September 20th. December 6, 13 and 20th.
Site Open: Easter to September, Sunday & Bank Holiday Mondays 11.00 to 17.30. Sundays October to March 12.00 to 17.00 (parties and special openings by arrangement).

What
Thomas Days   May 10th, July 19th, August 30 and 31st.
Model Railway Days   June 7th.
Transport Day   September 20th.
Santa Trains   December 6, 13 and 20th.

Where
LOCATION
Cheddleton Station, Nr Leek, Staffordshire ST13 7EE. Telephone (0538)360522. Sundays (0782)503458 Evenings.
ACCESS
By Bus: Cheddleton Service from Leek or Hanley.
By Road: 3 miles from Leek on A520.
By Rail: Stoke on Trent.
FACILITIES
Shop, Buffet, Museum, Car & Coach Parking, Picnic Area, Model Railway.
LOCOS
J94 Josiah Wedgwood, Ex-BR 2-6-4T 80136 (Under restoration), Ex-BR Class 08 D3420, Ex-LMS 4F 0-6-0 4422 (during 1992).
FARES
Steam days Adults 1.30, Child/O.A.P. 90p, Family (2 + 3) 4.50, static viewing Adult 70p, child/O.A.P. 50p.

Wilson's View
Restorers of one of Fowler's most noted designs, the Derby 4, the NSR also have a very handsome Jacobean-style station at Cheddleton, which is reputed to have been designed by Pugin. The Churnet valley, which is where the railway is situated, is an area of outstanding natural beauty and, in due course, the railway hope to extend along a seven-mile stretch of line through this splendid scenery.

The unique 8P and Blue Ribbon holder for the fastest climb from Appleby tNo 71000 Duke of Gloucester takes water at Didcot MPD. Photo Tony Jones.

North Yorkshire Moors Railway

When
Table A

Grosmont Dep	10.00	13.05	16.05	Pickering	Dep	11.15	14.50	17.20
Goathland Arr	10.10	13.18	16.18	Levisham	Arr	11.32	15.07	17.37
Goathland Dep	10.15	13.20	16.20	Levisham	Dep	11.33	15.08	17.38
Newtondale	10.29	13.34	16.34	Newtondale		11.44	15.19	17.49
Levisham Arr	10.39	13.44	16.44	Goathland	Arr	11.59	15.34	18.04
Levisham Dep	10.40	13.45	16.45	Goathland	Dep	12.01	15.36	18.05
Pickering Arr	10.57	14.02	17.02	Grosmont	Arr	12.11	15.46	18.15

Table B

Grosmont Dep	09.30	11.45	13.30	15.15	16.55
Goathland Arr	09.43	11.58	13.43	15.28	17.08
Goathland Dep	09.44	12.00	13.45	15.31	17.15
Newtondale	09.58	12.14	13.59	15.45	17.29
Levisham Arr	10.08	12.24	14.09	15.55	17.39
Levisham Dep	10.09	12.25	14.10	15.56	17.40
Pickering Arr	10.26	12.42	14.27	16.13	17.57
Pickering Dep	10.30	11.15	13.00	14.45	16.30
Levisham Arr	10.47	11.32	13.17	15.02	16.47
Levisham Dep	10.48	11.33	13.18	15.03	16.48
Newtondale	10.59	11.44	13.29	15.14	16.59
Goathland Arr	11.14	11.59	13.44	15.29	17.14
Goathland Dep	11.16	12.02	13.46	15.31	17.16
Grosmont Arr	11.26	12.12	13.56	15.41	17.26

Table C

Grosmont Dep	10.05	11.05	12.05	13.45	14.45	15.40	16.45
Goathland Arr	10.20	11.20	12.20	14.00	15.00	15.55	17.00
Goathland Dep	10.22	11.24	12.24	14.02	15.02	15.59	17.04
Newtondale	10.37	11.39	12.39	14.17	15.17	16.14	17.19
Levisham Arr	10.48	11.50	12.50	14.28	15.28	16.25	17.30
Levisham Dep	10.50	11.53	12.53	14.30	15.30	16.29	17.32
Pickering Arr	11.08	12.11	13.11	14.48	15.48	16.47	17.50

Pickering Dep	10.30	11.30	12.30	14.10	15.10	16.10	17.10
Levisham Arr	10.48	11.48	12.48	14.28	15.28	16.28	17.28
Levisham Dep	10.52	11.52	12.52	14.32	15.30	16.32	17.30
Newtondale	11.03	12.03	13.03	14.43	15.41	16.43	17.41
Goathland Arr	11.18	12.18	13.18	14.58	15.56	16.58	17.56
Goathland Dep	11.22	12.22	13.22	15.02	15.58	17.02	17.57
Grosmont Arr	11.36	12.36	13.36	15.12	16.08	17.12	18.07

Services Operate:

Table A: April 4,6-11,27-30th. May 1,8,9,15,16 and 22nd. September 8,19,21-26,28-30th. October 1,2,5-10,12-17,19-24 and 31st.

Table B: April 5,12-18,21-26th. May 2,5-7,10-14,17-21,23,29-31st. June 1-30th. July 1-12,18,24,25 and 31st. August 1,7,8,14,15,21,22,28 and 29th. September 4-17,20 and 27th. October 11,18,25-30th. November 1st.

Table C: April 19 and 20th. May 3,4,24-28th. July 13-16,19-23,26-30th. August 2-6,9-13,16-20,23-27,30 and 31st. September 1-3rd.

What

Diesel Day	May 9th (Table A applies, using Diesels).
25th Anniversary	June (various events throughout month, see press).
Steam Gala Weekend	October 3 and 4th (special timetable).
Santa Trains	December (phone for details & bookings).

Where

LOCATION

Pickering Station, Pickering, North Yorkshire. Telephone (0751)72508.

ACCESS

By Bus: United Serviced from Malton, York & Whitby.

By Road: Pickering is on A169/A170 in Pickering centre.

By Rail: Grosmont (interchange), Malton.

FACILITIES

Shop, Buffet, Car & coach parking, Railway Trail, Provision for Disabled, Pullman Wine & Dine (booking essential), Schools Advice Service.

LOCOS

Ex-LMS 4-6-0 45428 Eric Treacy, Ex-SR 4-6-0 841, Ex-GWR 0-6-2T 6619, Ex-BR 2-6-4T 80135, Lambton No5 0-6-2T, Ex-LNER 2-6-0 2005, Ex-WD Dame Vera Lynn, Ex-LNER 0-6-0T 60923 Joem, Ex-LNER Q7 3460, Diesels D821 Greyhound, D7628, 25191, D55009 Alycidon, D8568.

Wilson's View

This line across almost twenty miles of National Park is as much used by the hiking fraternity as it is by gricers, though there is a great deal here for the Railway Children. The shed at Grosmont is a treat and comes complete with its own coaling tower. There is the heavy one in forty-nine climb up the three and a half mile Goathland Bank, where the station, too, is a little gem. Add to this some unique motive power - the Raven Q7 No.901 and P3 No.2392, Thompson's K1 No.2005, Wordsell's J72 Joem supported and assisted by locos of the three other Grouping companies - and what you have is one of the finest preserved lines in the country.

Paignton & Dartmouth Railway

STANDARD GAUGE

When

Table A

		B	B	B	B
Paignton	Dep	10.30	12.15	14.15	16.15
Goodrington	Dep	10.35	12.20	14.20	16.20
Churston	Dep	10.45	12.30	14.30	16.30
Kingswear	Arr	11.00	12.45	14.45	16.45
Kingswear	Dep	11.15	12.55	15.15	17.00
Churston	Dep	11.30	13.10	15.30	17.15
Goodrington	Dep	11.40	13.20	15.40	17.25
Paignton	Arr	11.45	13.25	15.45	17.30

Table B

		B	B	B		
Paignton	Dep	10.15	11.35	13.30	14.50	16.15
Goodrington	Dep	10.20	11.40	13.35	14.55	16.20
Churston	Dep	10.30	11.50	13.45	15.05	16.30
Kingswear	Arr	10.45	12.05	14.00	15.20	16.45
Kingswear	Dep	10.55	12.15	14.10	15.30	17.00
Churston	Dep	11.10	12.30	14.25	15.45	17.15
Goodrington	Dep	11.20	12.40	14.35	15.55	17.25
Paignton	Arr	11.25	12.45	14.40	16.00	17.30

Table C

		B	B	B	B	B				
Paignton	Dep	10.15	11.00	11.45	12.30	14.00	14.45	15.30	16.15	17.00
Goodrington	Dep	10.20	11.05	11.50	12.35	14.05	14.50	15.35	16.20	17.05
Churston	Dep	10.30	11.15	12.00	12.45	14.15	15.00	15.45	16.30	17.15
Kingswear	Arr	10.45	11.30	12.15	13.00	14.30	15.15	16.00	16.45	17.30
Kingswear	Dep	10.15	11.00	11.45	12.30	13.15	14.00	14.45	15.30	16.15	17.00
Churston	Dep	10.30	11.15	12.00	12.45	13.30	14.15	15.00	15.45	16.30	17.15
Goodrington	Dep	10.40	11.25	12.10	12.55	13.40	14.25	15.10	15.55	16.40	17.25
Paignton	Arr	10.45	11.30	12.15	13.00	13.45	14.30	15.15	16.00	16.45	17.30

Note. (B) Boat Train Service, River Dart Boat Connections.

Service Operates:

Table A
April 5/12/17 to 23rd/28/30th. May Sundays Mondays Tuesdays and Thursdays from 3rd to 25th then daily until June 21st, June 27/28th then Saturdays & Sundays only in July, August & September. Sundays Tuesdays and Thursdays in October.

Table B
June 22nd to 26th/29/30, July 1st to 3rd/6th to 10th/13th to 17th. August 31st to September 4th/7th to 11th.

Table C
Mondays to Fridays July 24th to August 28th.

What

Luncheon Trains	Sundays April 12/26/May 10/24/June 7/28 September 13/27 October 11/25
Dining Trains	May 29th July 10/25 August 14/27/29th
Gala Weekend	June 20/21st
Halloween Special	October 29th
Santa Trains	December 5/6/12/13/17th to 24th Booking Recommended.

Where
LOCATION

Paignton & Dartmouth Steam Railway, Queens Park Station, Paignton TQ4 6AF.
Telephone(0803)555872.

ACCESS

By Bus: Torquay/Paignton served from most major cities, local services from Torquay, bus link with Totnes.

By Road: Paignton is on A385 from Totnes.

By Rail: Paignton, this is a shared station.

FACILITIES

Shop, Buffet, River Cruise, River Link to Totnes Return via Bus, Goodrington Station gives access directly to Goodrington Sands.

LOCOS

Locos inter-change with those on Dart Valley, usually Ex-GWR 2-6-2T Nos 4555, 4588, and Ex-GWR 4-6-0 7827 Lydham Manor.

Wilson's View

From the golden beaches of Goodrington Sands, under Agatha Christie's house, to the banks of the picturesque Dart, this line is a classic, tunnels and viaducts, inclines and cuttings are all to be found here. From the brash bright lights of Paignton the steam train will haul you back through time to the cultured calm of historic Dartmouth, via Kingswear.

Peak Rail

STANDARD GAUGE

When

Steam Centre 10.00 to 17.00 Daily except Christmas & New Year.

Note: These are 1991 details, no update received for 1992. Phone before travelling.

Where
LOCATION

Matlock Station, Matlock, Derbyshire. Buxton Midland Station, Buxton, Derbyshire.
Telephone (0629)580381 or (0298)79898.

ACCESS

By Bus: National Bus to Matlock or Buxton.

By Road: Both Buxton and Matlock are on the A6.

By Rail: Buxton via Manchester (Piccadilly). Matlock via Derby (Not Sundays).

FACILITIES

Buxton: Shop, Buffet, Car Parking.

Matlock: Shop, Buffet, Car Parking.

Wilson's View

This line could become one of the giants, though as yet they are only operating on the stretch from Matlock to Darley Dale. The ultimate aim is to reopen the complete line from Matlock to Buxton right through the heart of the Peak District National Park. Having secured the Matlock Darley section, the faithful volunteers are now working toward Rowsley where, as I recall, there is a genuine loco shed.

Plym Valley Railway

When
No details received for 1992, phone before travelling.

Where
LOCATION
Marsh Hills Station, Coypool, Plymouth, Devon PL7 4NL.
Telephone: (0752) 330478.
ACCESS
By Bus: Local services from Plymouth town centre.
By Road: Off A38 on north side of Plymouth town centre at Marsh Mills Roundabout take the Plympton exit & Colypool Road is 2nd left.
By Rail: Plymouth.
FACILITIES
Shop, Buffet.

Wilson's View
Years of hard work on a greenfield site and the tackling of a major restoration - on 34007 Wadebridge - have both been beset by difficulties. However, the volunteers are now beginning to see a glimmer of light at the end of the tunnel.

Pontypool & Blaenavon Railway

When
Service Operates: Frequently between 12.00 to 17.00.
March 1st, April 19th/20th, Sundays April 26th to August 30th, All Bank Holiday Mondays.

What
St David's Day	March 1st
Thomas Weekend	July 4th/5th
Santa Trains	December 5/6/12/13/19/20th

Where
LOCATION
Near Big Pit Museum, Blaenavon, Gwent.
Telephone(0495)772726 (Evenings only).
ACCESS
By Bus: Blaenavon-Brynmawr service.
By Road: From Pontypool A4043 and B4248 or B4248 off A465. Abergavenny/Tredegar Road.
By Rail: Pontypool or Abergavenny.
FACILITIES
Light Refreshments, Souvenirs, Car & Coach Parking.

Wilson's View
Set in an almost lunar landscape, the P & BR gives the visitor some idea of the awesome scale of mining operations in the Welsh Valleys. Indeed, the railway forms part of the attractions of the Big Pit complex, a museum of mining based in a redundant coal mine. In addition to the line's working industrial locos, there are also several ex-GWR mainline locos on display - they are in more or less ex-Barry condition, though some basic cosmetic work has been carried out.

Ravenglass & Eskdale Railway

NARROW GAUGE

When

Table A

		D				D
Eskdale	Dep	07.45		Ravenglass	Dep	16.30
Beckfoot		P.U.		Muncaster		16.35
The Green		07.55		Irton Road		16.50
Irton Road		08.00		The Green		16.54
Muncaster		08.13		Beckfoot		S.D.
Ravenglass	Arr	08.20		Dalegarth		17.05

Table B

		H	HB	C	D
Ravenglass	Dep	12.00	14.00	14.20	16.30
Muncaster		12.05	14.05	14.25	16.36
Irton Road		12.20	14.20	14.40	16.50
The Green		12.25	14.25	14.45	16.55
Beckfoot		TRAINS SET DOWN ONLY			
Eskdale	Arr	12.40	14.40	15.00	17.05

		DMFO	DSSO	B	C	B	C
Eskdale	Dep	07.30	10.00	13.00	13.20	15.00	15.20
Beckfoot		07.32	10.02	TRAINS PICK UP ONLY			
The Green		07.40	10.13	13.11	13.33	15.11	15.33
Irton Road		07.45	10.20	13.15	13.38	15.15	15.38
Muncaster		07.58	10.33	13.28	13.53	15.28	15.53
Ravenglass	Arr	08.05	10.40	13.35	14.00	15.35	16.00

Table C

		D	SX			D				D
Ravenglass	Dep	09.00	10.00	11.00	12.00	13.00	14.00	15.00	16.00	17.00
Muncaster		09.05	10.05	11.05	12.05	13.05	14.05	15.05	16.05	17.05
Irton Road		09.20	10.20	11.20	12.20	13.20	14.20	15.20	16.20	17.20
The Green		09.24	10.25	11.25	12.25	13.25	14.25	15.25	16.25	17.25
Beckfoot		S.D.	S.D.	S.D.	S.D.	S.D.	S.D.	S.D.	S.D.	S.D.
Eskdale	Arr	09.35	10.40	11.40	12.40	13.40	14.40	15.40	16.40	17.40

		DSUX	D	SX			D			
Eskdale	Dep	07.45	10.00	11.00	12.00	13.20	14.00	15.00	16.00	17.00
Beckfoot		07.47	10.02	P.U.	P.U.	P.U.	P.U.	P.U.	P.U.	P.U.
The Green		07.55	10.13	11.13.	12.13	13.33	14.13	15.13	16.13	17.13
Irton Road		08.00	10.20	11.20	12.20	13.38	14.20	15.20	16.20	17.20
Muncaster		08.13	10.33	11.33	12.33	13.53	14.33	15.33	16.33	17.33
Ravenglass	Arr	08.20	10.40	11.40	12.40	14.00	14.40	15.40	16.40	17.40

Table D

		D						D
Ravenglass	Dep	09.00	11.10	12.00	13.00	14.20	15.40	16.30
Muncaster		09.05	11.15	12.05	13.05	14.25	15.45	16.35
Irton Road		09.20	11.30	12.20	13.20	14.40	16.00	16.50
The Green		09.24	11.35	12.25	13.25	14.45	16.05	16.55
Beckfoot		S.D.	S.D.	S.D.	S.D.	S.D.	S.D.	S.D.
Eskdale	Arr	09.35	11.50	12.40	13.40	15.00	16.20	17.05

		DSUX	D					
Eskdale	Dep	07.30	10.00	12.00	13.20	14.40	15.20	16.35
Beckfoot		07.32	10.02	P.U.	P.U.	P.U.	P.U.	P.U.
The Green		07.40	10.13	12.13	13.33	14.53	15.33	16.45
Irton Road		07.45	10.20	12.20	13.38	14.58	15.38	16.50
Muncaster		07.58	10.33	12.33	13.53	15.13	15.53	17.03
Ravenglass	Arr	08.05	10.40	12.40	14.00	15.20	16.00	17.10

Table E

		D	SX			AMTO		D	
Ravenglass	Dep	09.00	10.00	11.00	11.40	12.00	12.20	13.00	13.40
Muncaster		09.05	10.05	11.05	11.45	12.05	12.25	13.05	13.45
Irton Road		09.20	10.20	11.20	12.00	12.20	12.40	13.20	14.00
The Green		09.24	10.25	11.25	12.05	12.25	12.45	13.25	14.05
Beckfoot		TRAINS STOP AT BECKFOOT TO SET DOWN ONLY							
Eskdale	Arr	09.35	10.40	11.40	12.20	12.40	13.00	13.40	14.20

		DSX	D	SX				AMTO	D
Eskdale	Dep	07.45	10.00	11.00	12.00	12.40	13.20	13.40	14.00
Beckfoot		07.47	10.02	TRAINS STOP HERE TO PICK UP ONLY					
The Green		07.55	10.13	11.13	12.13	12.53	13.33	13.53	14.13
Irton Road		08.00	10.20	11.18	12.18	12.58	13.38	13.58	14.18
Muncaster		08.13	10.33	11.33	12.33	13.13	13.53	14.13	14.33
Ravenglass	Arr	08.20	10.40	11.40	12.40	13.20	14.00	14.20	14.40

			AFSX				X	A	
Ravenglass	Dep	14.20	14.40	15.00	15.40	16.20	17.25	18.50	
Muncaster		14.25	14.45	15.05	15.45	16.25	17.30	18.55	
Irton Road		14.40	15.00	15.20	16.00	16.40	17.45	19.10	
The Green		14.45	15.05	15.25	16.05	16.45	17.54	19.14	
Beckfoot		TRAINS STOP AT BECKFOOT TO SET DOWN ONLY							
Eskdale	Arr	15.00	15.20	15.40	16.20	17.00	18.00	19.35	

			AFSX					X	
Eskdale	Dep	14.40	15.20	15.40	16.00	16.40	17.25	18.10	
Beckfoot		TRAINS STOP HERE TO PICK UP ONLY							
The Green		14.53	15.33	15.53	16.13	16.53	17.38	18.20	
Irton Road		14.58	15.38	15.58	16.18	16.58	17.45	18.25	
Muncaster		15.13	15.53	16.13	16.33	17.13	17.58	18.38	
Ravenglass	Arr	15.20	16.00	16.20	16.40	17.20	18.05	18.45	

Yes it is a steam locomotive. The Middletown Railway's mobile tea urn - Sentinel No 54 clags her way on the GN curve.

Table F

		D		D		D	D
Ravenglass	Dep	10.40	12.00	13.20	14.20	15.20	16.20
Muncaster		10.45	12.05	13.25	14.25	15.25	16.25
Irton Road		11.00	12.20	13.40	14.40	15.40	16.40
The Green		11.05	12.25	13.45	14.45	15.43	16.44
Beckfoot		SETS DOWN ONLY					
Eskdale	Arr	11.20	12.40	14.00	15.00	15.53	16.55

		SX	D		D		D
Eskdale	Dep	07.45	11.40	13.20	14.20	15.20	16.20
Beckfoot		07.47	PICKS UP ONLY				
The Green		07.55	11.53	13.33	14.33	15.33	16.30
Irton Road		08.00	11.58	13.40	14.40	15.38	16.35
Muncaster		08.13	12.13	13.53	14.53	15.53	16.48
Ravenglass	Arr	08.20	12.20	14.00	15.00	16.00	16.55

Notes:
A. Runs July 20th to August 27th.
B. Saturdays & Sundays only February 15th to March 22nd.
C. Runs March 28th to May 9th, excluding April 17th to 20th & May 2nd to 4th.
H. Under normal circumstances steam operated. D. Diesel hauled.
X. Diesel operated until July 20th and from September 6th.
SX. Sundays excepted. MTO. Monday to Thursday only. FSX. Fridays and Saturdays excepted.
MFO. Mondays to Fridays only.

Service Operates:
Table A :Monday to Friday only January 6th to March 29th. From November 2nd to December.
Table B :Saturdays and Sundays Only. February 15th to March 29th, daily March 30th to May 11th. Except Easter (April 17th to 26th). and May Day Holiday (May 2nd-4th). The 12.00 and 14.00 Ex-Ravenglass and the 13.00 and 15.00 Ex-Eskdale also run Saturdays and Sundays 1st-15th November and daily December 26th to January 1st 1993.
Table C :May 11th to July 18th, September 4th to 28th (excluding May 23rd-25th).
Table D :Easter April 17th to 26th, May Day 2nd to 4th.
Table E :May 23rd to 25th and July 19th to September 3rd.
Table F :September 29th to November 1st.

Where

LOCATION
Ravenglass, Cumbria CA18 1SW
Telephone (0229) 717171
ACCESS
By Bus: Ravenglass Services from Barrow and Whitehaven.
By Road: Via A595 Barrow/Whitehaven Road.
By Rail: Ravenglass (connecting services).
FACILITIES
Shop, Buffet, Bar Meals in 'Ratty Arms' (Ravenglass), Museum.
Car & Coach Parking, Provision For Disabled, Camping Coaches.
LOCOS
Northern Rock, River Irt, River Mite, Diesel, Shelagh of Eskdale.

Wilson's View

The Ratty is one of the most scenic fifteen-inch gauge lines in the country. It is also a public service railway, with train services throughout the year providing connections with the BR network. The railway has its own workshops which have built locomotives and coaches, some for export. At Muncaster, the railway bought and restored to operational use an old water mill - the flour that it now mills is on sale in the railway's shops.

Romney Hythe & Dymchurch Railway

NARROW GAUGE

When

Hythe	Dep	10.30	12.00	14.00	15.20	16.45	18.00	Saturdays and Sundays
Dymchurch		10.48	12.18	14.18	15.38	17.03	18.18	February 29th to April 5th
Jstonelane		10.53	12.23	14.23	15.43	17.08	18.23	October 3rd to Nov 1st
New Romney	Arr	11.05	12.35	14.35	15.55	17.20	18.35	Daily April 27th to May 1st
New Romney	Dep	11.08	12.38	14.38	15.58	-	-	May 5th to 22nd &
Romney S		11.20	12.50	14.50	16.10	-	-	Sept 28th to Oct 2nd
Dungeness	Arr	11.35	13.05	15.05	16.25	-	-	

Dungeness	Dep	-	-	12.05	13.35	15.25	16.50
Romney S		-	-	12.20	13.50	15.40	17.05
New Romney	Arr	-	-	12.33	14.03	15.53	17.18
New Romney	Dep	09.35	11.05	12.35	14.05	15.55	17.20
Jstonelane		09.43	11.13	12.43	14.13	16.03	17.28
Dymchurch		09.50	11.20	12.50	14.20	16.10	17.35
Hythe	Arr	10.10	11.40	13.10	14.40	16.30	17.55

Mondays to Fridays on the daily dates above

Hythe	Dep	11.15	14.30	17.30
Dymchurch		11.33	14.48	17.48
Jstonelane		11.38	14.53	17.53
New Romney	Arr	11.50	15.05	18.05
New Romney	Dep	11.53	15.08	-
Romney S		12.05	15.20	-
Dungeness	Arr	12.20	15.35	-

Dungeness	Dep	-	12.50	16.05
Romney S		-	13.05	16.20
New Romney	Arr	-	13.18	16.33
New Romney	Dep	10.00	13.20	16.35
Jstonelane		10.08	13.28	16.43
Dymchurch		10.15	13.35	16.50
Hythe	Arr	10.35	13.55	17.10

Daily April 11th to 16th & 21st to 26th, June 1st to July 21st, September 7th to 27th.

Hythe	Dep	10.30	11.30	12.30	13.30	14.30	15.30	16.30	17.30	18.30
Dymchurch		10.48	11.48	12.48	13.48	14.48	15.48	16.48	17.48	18.48
Jstonelane		10.53	11.43	12.53	13.53	14.53	15.53	16.53	17.53	18.53
New Romney	Arr	11.05	12.05	13.05	14.05	15.05	16.05	17.05	18.05	19.05
New Romney	Dep	11.08	12.08	13.08	14.08	15.08	16.08	-	18.08A	-
Romney S		11.20	12.20	13.20	14.20	15.20	16.20	-	18.20A	-
Dungeness	Arr	11.35	12.35	13.35	14.35	15.35	16.35	-	-	-

Dungeness	Dep	-	-	-	12.05	13.05	14.05	15.05	16.05	17.05
Romney S		-	10.20	-	12.20	13.20	14.20	15.20	16.20	17.20
New Romney	Arr	-	10.33	-	12.33	13.33	14.33	15.33	16.33	17.33
New Romney	Dep	09.35	10.35	11.35	12.35	13.35	14.35	15.35	16.35	17.35
Jstonelane		09.43	10.43	11.43	12.43	13.43	14.43	15.43	16.43	17.43
Dymchurch		09.50	10.50	11.50	12.50	13.50	14.50	15.50	16.50	17.50
Hythe	Arr	10.10	11.10	12.10	13.10	14.10	15.10	16.10	17.10	18.10

Daily April 17th to 20th, May 2nd to 4th & 23rd to 31st, July 22nd to September 6th

Hythe	Dep	10.20	11.05	11.50	12.35	13.20	14.05
Dymchurch	Dep	10.38	11.23	12.08	12.53	13.38	14.23
Jstonelane	Dep	10.43	11.28	12.13	12.58	13.43	14.28
New Romney	Arr	10.55	11.40	12.25	13.10	13.55	14.40
New Romney	Dep	10.58	11.43	12.28	13.13	13.58	14.43
Romney S	Dep	11.10	11.55	12.40	13.25	14.10	14.55
Dungeness	Arr	11.25	12.10	12.55	13.40	14.25	15.10

Hythe	Dep	14.50	15.35	16.20	17.05	17.30	18.15
Dymchurch	Dep	15.08	15.53	16.38	17.23	17.48	18.33
Jstonelane	Dep	15.13	15.58	16.43	17.28	17.53	18.38
New Romney	Arr	15.25	16.10	16.55	17.40	18.05	18.50
New Romney	Dep	15.28	16.13	16.58	-	19.08A	
Romney S	Dep	15.40	16.25	17.10	-	18.20A	
Dungeness	Arr	15.55	17.25	-	-	-	

Dungeness	Dep	-	-	-	-	11.40	12.25
Romney S	Dep	-	-	10.40	-	11.55	12.40
New Romney	Arr	-	-	10.53	-	12.08	12.53
New Romney	Dep	09.25	10.10	10.55	11.40	12.10	12.55
Jstonelane	Dep	09.33	10.18	11.03	11.48	12.18	13.03
Dymchurch	Dep	09.40	10.25	11.10	11.55	12.25	13.10
Hythe	Arr	10.00	10.45	11.30	12.15	12.45	13.30

Dungeness	Dep	13.10	13.55	14.20	15.25	16.10	16.55	17.40
Romney S	Dep	13.25	14.10	14.55	15.40	16.25	17.10	17.55
New Romney	Arr	13.38	14.23	15.08	15.43	16.38	17.23	18.08
New Romney	Dep	13.40	14.25	15.10	15.55	16.40	17.25	18.10
Jstonelane	Dep	13.48	14.33	15.18	16.03	16.48	17.33	18.18
Dymchurch	Dep	13.55	14.40	15.25	16.10	16.55	17.40	18.25
Hythe	Arr	14.15	15.00	15.45	16.30	17.15	18.00	18.45

Saturdays only April 17th to 20th, May 2nd to 4th & 23rd to 31st, July 22nd to September 6th.

Hythe	Dep	13.20	14.05	14.20	15.20	16.20	16.40	17.20	18.20
Dymchurch		13.38		14.38	15.38	16.28	16.58	17.38	18.38
Jstonelane		13.43		14.43	15.43	16.43	17.03	17.43	18.43
New Romney	Arr	13.55		14.55	15.55	16.55	17.15	17.55	18.55
New Romney	Dep	13.58		14.58	15.58	16.58		17.58A	
Romney S		14.10		15.10	16.10	17.10		18.10A	
Dungeness	Arr	14.25	14.50	15.25	16.25	17.25		18.25A	

Dungeness	Dep	14.55	15.35	15.55	16.55	17.55
Romney S		15.10		16.10	17.10	18.10
New Romney	Arr	15.23		16.23	17.23	18.23
New Romney	Dep	15.25		16.25	17.25	18.25
Jstonelane		15.33		16.33	17.33	18.33
Dymchurch		15.40		16.40	17.40	18.40
Hythe	Arr	16.00	16.20	17.00	18.00	19.00

Notes: A Runs if required by holders of return tickets issued at Romney Sands or Dungeness.

What

Steam & Diesel Gala	May 17th
Bus Rally	June 21st
Romney on Parade	September 13th

Where
LOCATION
Romney Hythe & Dymchurch Railway, New Romney Station, Kent. Telephone (0679)62353.
ACCESS
By Bus: From Folkestone East Kent Services to Hythe.
By Road: Off A259 at New Romney.
By Rail: Folkestone or Sanding Junction.
FACILITIES
Shop, Buffet, Model Railway, Car & Coach Parking, Observation Coach.
FARES
Not Advised.
LOCOS
Hurricane, Samson, Southern Maid, Green Goddess. Dr Syn, The Bug, Typhoon.

Wilson's View
This fifteen-inch gauge line is, like the Ravenglass and Eskdale, a public service railway. It operates to the highest standards of railway practice and, with its fleet of Greenley designed 4-6-2s and 2-8-2s, bears a striking resemblance to the old Late Never Early, or the London and Nearly Everywhere, as it was known by its admirers - more correctly, the London and North Eastern Railway. The railway also operates School Trains, having won the local contract against stiff opposition from the Bus companies - how often has the reverse been true?

Rutland Railway Museum

STANDARD GAUGE

When
No details were received from this site but contact details have been included. Intending visitors should draw their own conclusions and try to contact the line before making any visits.

Where
LOCATION
Rutland Railway Museum, Ashwell Road, Cottesmore, Nr.Oakham.
Leicestershire.
Telephone (0572)813203 or (0780)62384.
ACCESS
By Bus: Blands-Leicester-Oakham-Cottesmore. Bartons-Services 117,125 from Nottingham, Melton Mowbray, Ashwell, Corby, P/Borough.
By Road: Off A1 between Stamford & Grantham on B668 at Cottesmore.
By Rail: Oakham (4 miles) taxi service available. Classic buses operate from Oakham to the site on ironstone and steam gala weekends.
FACILITIES
Shop, Buffet, Car Parking, Lineside Walk, Picnic Area.
LOCOS
0-4-0ST Singapore, 0-4-0ST Dora, 0-6-0ST Salmon, Diesels D9520,D9555, Betty, NCP No.1, Colsterworth, Phoenix, 219001.

Wilson's View
Based on a former iron stone line, the Rutland Railway Museum recreates the scene of the industrial railway. In its early days, the Rutland Railway Museum was involved with tour operators FSS, and both Flying Scotsman herself and Pendennis Castle were amongst the locos stored at the Quarry complex at Market Overton. Volunteers from these early beginnings became the backbone of the RRM. In addition to the recreation of the industrial railway, the museum is also the custodian of a very rare old coach - the last survivor from the Wisbech and Upwell Tramway. The society believe they have the largest collection of goods wagons in the country - over eighty of them.

Severn Valley Railway

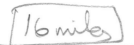

STANDARD GAUGE

When

Table A

Kidderminster	Dep	10.45	12.45	14.45	16.55
Bewdley	Arr	10.57	12.57	14.57	17.07
Bewdley	Dep	11.00	13.00	15.00	17.12
Arley	Arr	11.13	13.13	15.13	17.25
Arley	Dep	11.15	13.15	15.15	17.27
Highley	Arr	11.23	13.23	15.23	17.35
Highley	Dep	11.25	13.25	15.25	17.37
Hampton Loade	Arr	11.33	13.33	15.33	17.45
Hampton Loade	Dep	11.37	13.37	15.37	17.47
Bridgnorth	Arr	11.54	13.54	15.54	18.04
Bridgnorth	Dep	11.15	13.15	15.15	16.15
Hampton Loade	Arr	11.32	13.32	15.32	16.32
Hampton Loade	Dep	11.37	13.37	15.37	16.35
Highley	Arr	11.45	13.45	15.45	16.43
Highley	Dep	11.47	13.47	15.47	16.45
Arley	Arr	11.55	13.55	15.55	16.53
Arley	Dep	11.57	13.57	15.57	16.55
Bewdley	Arr	12.10	14.10	16.10	17.08
Bewdley	Dep	12.13	14.13	16.13	17.13
Kidderminster	Arr	12.25	14.25	16.25	17.25

Table B

Station				RS				
Kidderminster	Dep	10.20	11.40	12.15	12.55	14.10	15.25	16.40
Bewdley	Arr	10.32	11.52		13.07	14.22	15.37	16.52
Bewdley	Dep	10.40	11.55		13.10	14.25	15.40	16.55
Arley	Arr	10.53	12.08		13.23	14.38	15.53	17.08
Arley	Dep	10.56	12.11		13.26	14.41	15.56	17.10
Highley	Arr	11.04	12.19		13.34	14.49	16.04	17.19
Highley	Dep	11.07	12.22		13.37	14.52	16.07	17.21
Hampton Loade	Arr	11.15	12.30		13.45	15.00	16.15	17.29
Hampton Loade	Dep	11.18	12.33		13.48	15.03	16.18	17.32
Bridgnorth	Arr	11.35	12.50	13.24	14.05	15.20	16.35	17.49

Station					RS			
Bridgnorth	Dep	10.55	12.10	13.25	14.08	14.40	15.55	17.10
Hampton Loade	Arr	11.12	12.27	13.42		14.57	16.12	17.27
Hampton Loade	Dep	11.17	12.32	13.47		15.02	16.17	17.31
Highley	Arr	11.25	12.40	13.55		15.10	16.25	17.39
Highley	Dep	11.28	12.43	13.58		15.13	16.28	17.41
Arley	Arr	11.36	12.51	14.06		15.21	16.36	17.50
Arley	Dep	11.39	12.54	14.09		15.24	16.39	17.52
Bewdley	Arr	11.52	13.07	14.22		15.37	16.52	18.05
Bewdley	Dep	11.55	13.10	14.25		15.40	16.55	18.08
Kidderminster	Arr	12.07	13.22	14.37	15.17	15.52	17.07	18.18

Table C

				R							
Kidderminster	Dep	10.35	11.15	11.55	12.40	13.25	14.10	14.55	15.40	16.25	17.10
Bewdley	Arr	10.46	11.26	12.06	12.51	13.36	14.21	15.06	15.51	16.36	17.21
Bewdley	Dep	10.50	11.30	12.14	12.59	13.44	14.29	15.14	15.59	16.44	17.29
Arley	Arr	11.04	11.44	12.28	13.13	13.58	14.43	15.28	16.13	16.58	17.43
Arley	Dep	11.06	11.49	12.33	13.18	14.03	14.48	15.33	16.18	17.03	17.48
Highley	Arr	11.15	11.58	12.42	13.27	14.12	14.57	15.42	16.27	17.12	17.57
Highley	Dep	11.17	12.02	12.46	13.31	14.16	15.01	15.46	16.31	17.16	18.01
Hampton L.	Arr	11.25	12.10	12.54	13.39	14.24	15.09	15.54	16.39	17.24	18.09
Hampton L.	Dep	11.28	12.13	12.57	13.42	14.27	15.12	15.57	16.42	17.27	18.12
Bridgnorth	Arr	11.45	12.30	13.14	13.59	14.44	15.29	16.14	16.59	17.44	18.29

					R						
Bridgnorth	Dep	11.05	11.50	12.35	13.20	14.05	14.50	15.35	16.20	17.05	17.50
Hampton L.	Arr	11.22	12.07	12.52	13.37	14.22	15.07	15.52	16.37	17.22	18.07
Hampton L.	Dep	11.27	12.12	12.57	13.42	14.27	15.12	15.57	16.42	17.27	18.12
Highley	Arr	11.35	12.20	13.05	13.50	14.35	15.20	16.05	16.50	17.35	18.20
Highley	Dep	11.39	12.24	13.09	13.54	14.39	15.24	16.09	16.54	17.39	18.23
Arley	Arr	11.47	12.32	13.17	14.02	14.47	15.32	16.17	17.02	17.47	18.31
Arley	Dep	11.50	12.37	13.22	14.07	14.52	15.37	16.22	17.07	17.52	18.33
Bewdley	Arr	12.03	12.50	13.35	14.20	15.05	15.50	16.35	17.20	18.05	18.46
Bewdley	Dep	12.07	12.54	13.39	14.24	15.09	15.54	16.39	17.24	18.09	18.48
Kidderminster	Arr	12.19	13.06	13.51	14.36	15.21	16.06	16.51	17.36	18.21	19.00

Table D

Bridgnorth	Dep	12.00	13.30	15.00	Highley	Dep	12.40	14.10	15.40
Hampton L.	Arr	12.15	13.45	15.15	Hampton L.	Arr	12.48	14.18	15.48
Hampton L.	Dep	12.17	13.47	15.17	Hampton L.	Dep	12.50	14.20	15.50
Highley	Arr	12.25	13.55	15.25	Bridgnorth	Arr	13.05	14.35	16.05

This table is a guide to the winter timetable, see notes for service dates.

Notes: (R) Sunday luncheon service (booking essential). (RS) Severn Valley Ltd Sunday service (does not call at intermediate stations, booking essential).

Services Operate:
Table A: March 16th. April 22-24th. May 11-15th, 17-22nd. Mondays to Fridays: June 1st to July 17th, September 7th to October 2nd, October 19-23rd.

Table B: March 17,21,22 and 28th. April 4,5,17,18,21,25 and 26th. May 2,3,9,10,16,23,26-31st. June 13,14,20,27 and 28th. July 4,5,11 and 12th, then Monday to Saturday until September 6th. September 12,13,19 and 20th. October 3,4,10,17,18 and 31st. November 1st.

Table C: May 4,24 and 25th. July 26th. August 2,9,16,23,30 and 31st.

Special timetables apply on March 29th, June 6-7th, June 21st, October 11, 24 and 25th. Winter service on November 7,8,14,15,21,22,28 and 29th. Santa service commences December 5-6th.

TableD: A Western Diesel will be in operation on May 2nd, June 13th, July 4th, August 8th and September 5th.

What

Spring Steam Gala	April 11-12th.
Diesel Gala	May (not confirmed)
Freight Workings	June 6-7th.
Fathers Day	June 21st.
Autumn Steam Gala	September 26-27th.
Vintage Vehicle Day	October 11th.
Diesel Gala	October 24-25th.
Santa Trains	December 5 and 6th to Xmas Eve.

Christmas luncheon service on last wekend in November (booking essential)
Special timetables apply on above services.

Where

LOCATION

The Railway Station, Bewdley, Worcester DT12 1BG. Telephone (0299) 403816 or (0746) 764361.

ACCESS

By Bus: Midland Red West and West Midland Travel run services from Birmingham, Wolverhampton and other West Midland towns to Bridgnorth, Bewdley and Kidderminster.

By Road: Kidderminster is on the A448 Kidderminster to Bromsgrove road. Bewdley is off the A456 Birmingham to Leominster road and Bridgnorth is off the A458 Birmingham to Shrewsbury road.

By Rail: Kidderminster, BR connection.

FACILITIES

Shops, Buffet, Restaurant, Sunday Lunch Trains (booking essential), Through fares from BR, Model Railway (Bewdley) Provision for Disabled, Car & Coach Parking, Picnic Area (Arley) Real Ale Bars (Kidderminster and Bridgnorth).

LOCOS

Ex-GWR's 2-8-0 2857, 2-6-2T 4566, 4-6-0 6960 Raveningham Hall, 0-6-0PT 7714, 4-6-0 7819 Hinton Manor. Ex-LMS' 2-6-0 2968, 0-6-0T 47383, 2-6-0 46443, 5XP 4-6-0 Leander, 2-8-0 8233. Ex-LNER 2-6-0 3442 Great Marquess. Ex-BR 4-6-0 75069 and Ex-SR 4-6-2 34027 Taw Valley. Expected to enter service in 1992 are Ex-GWR 0-6-0PT 3612 and 2-6-0 9303.

Wilson's View

The Severn Valley is undoubtedly the most commercial of all the preserved lines. Under the leadership of its General Manager, Michael Draper, the SVR has grown to become one of the leading tourist attractions in the country. The sixteen-mile route has all the right ingredients with splendid scenery, charming country station, an impressive loco fleet and even its own boiler shop. The railway carries over two hundred thousand passengers, and its twice-yearly Galas often see ten or more locomotives in action and more than a dozen services a day in each direction, including a late night special, which arrives back at Bridgnorth after all good Railway Children should really be in bed!

———— **SIDE TIPPING WAGON** ————

Sittingbourne & Kemsley Light Railway

When
No details received from this site but contact details have been included. Intending visitors should draw their own conclusions and try to contact the line before making any visits.

Where
LOCATION
The Wall, Milton Regis, Sittingbourne, Kent.
Telephone (0795)424899(Talking Timetable) Enquiries (0634)52672.
ACCESS
By Bus: Sittingbourne services from Maidstone or London.
By Road: A2 or M2 site is near town centre behind the B.R. Station.
By Rail: Sittingbourne.
FACILITIES
Shop, Buffet, Picnic Area, No Public Access by road To Kemsley Down.
FARES
Day Rover Adult 3.00 Child 1.50, Ord Return 1.80, Child 90p, Senior Citizen 1.30, Family Two Adults and up to Four children 5.00.
LOCOS
Premier, Triumph, Superb, Diesel Victor.

Wilson's View
One of the very early preservation pioneers, the S&KLR utilises motive power built for the line, which was part of the operations of a local paper manufacturer, Edward Lloyd. The line still skirts the factory as it leaves Sittingbourne for its journey across the Downs to Kemsley where the workshops and museum are situated. Access to Kemsley is by train only. The line is to the gauge of two foot six inches, and the locomotives in use are from the well known Kerr Stuart or Bagnall loco building companies.

Snowdon Mountain Railway

When
Weather permitting, and if there are at least 25 passengers, the first trains depart from Llanberis at 09.00 (08.30 in August). Trains run at frequent intervals until mid/late afternoon.
At peak periods, Bank Holidays and mid-July to early September, trains depart every 30 minutes until 17.30 and Saturdays until 15.30. The company uses its best endeavours to run at least the 09.30, 11.30 and 13.30 on all service days. The line is open daily March 15th to November 1st.

Where
LOCATION
Llanberis, Nr Caernarfon, Gwynedd LL55 4TY. Telephone (0286)870223.
ACCESS
By Bus: BWS Gwynedd from Caernarfon.
By Road: A4086 Caernarfon/Betws-y-Coed Road.
By Rail: Bangor(Then bus to Caernarfon).
FACILITIES
Shop, Buffet, Car & Coach Parking, Some Provision for Disabled, All inclusive coach tours run to the line from Llandudno and Pwllheli.
LOCOS
0-4-2TS No2 Enid, No3 Wyddfa, No4 Snowdon, No5 Moel Siabod, No6 Padarn, No7 Ralph Sadler and No8 Eryri plus 3 purpose built diesels.

Wilson's View
Britain's only Rack railway, the Snowdon Mountain is still using the Swiss-built locos which were supplied new to the railway on its opening in 1896. For the past ninety-six years, these powerful little 0-4-2s have pushed their coach up gradients of one in five, past grazing sheep and back-pack hikers to within a few feet of the top of Snowdon. The view is one thing, the barking exhausts are something else!

South Devon Railway

STANDARD GAUGE

When

Table A

					X	Y	X
Buckfastleigh	Dep	11.00	12.20	14.00	15.10	15.30	16.15
Staverton	Dep	11.13	12.33	14.13	15.23	15.43	16.28
Littlehempston	Arr	11.23	12.43	14.23	15.33	15.53	16.38
					X	Y	X
Littlehempston	Dep	11.32	12.52	14.32	15.42	16.02	16.47
Staverton	Dep	11.42	13.02	14.42	15.52	16.12	16.57
Buckfastleigh	Arr	11.55	13.15	14.55	16.05	16.25	17.10

Table B

Buckfastleigh	Dep	11.45	13.30	15.30
Staverton	Dep	11.58	13.43	15.43
Littlehempston	Arr	12.08	13.53	15.53
Littlehempston	Dep	12.17	14.02	16.02
Staverton	Dep	12.27	14.12	16.12
Buckfastleigh	Arr	12.40	14.25	16.25

Notes: (X) does not run April 21-23rd, May 26-28th, June, July (except 26 to 30th), Fridays & Saturdays in August or after September 4th.
(Y) runs on dates in Table A when (X) is not running. DMU service on Saturdays April 4,11th and May 9,16 and 23rd.

Service Operates:
Table A: March 29th. April 21,22 and 23rd. May 24-28th. June 21-25th and 28-30th. July 1,2,5-9,12-16,19-23 and 26-30th. Daily in August except Saturdays. September 1-4,6,13,20 and 27th. October 4th.
Table B: March 29th. April 1,4,5,8,11,12,15-18,24-26 and 29th. May 2,6,9,10,13,16,17,20,23 and 29-31st. June 1-20,26 and 27th. July 3,4,10,11,17,18,24,25 and 31st. August, Saturdays only. September 5th then daily to 30th (Sundays excepted). October 3,7,10,11,14,17,18,20-22,25 and 28th.
Services also run on April 19 and 20th, May 3 and 4th at the following times: 10.30 11.40 12.50 14.00 15.10 and 16.15. Intermediate timings are as per Tables A&B.

What
Santa Trains run December 5,6,12,13,19 and 20th.

Where
LOCATION
Buckfastleigh Station, Buckfastleigh, Devon. Telephone (0364) 42338
ACCESS
By Road: Buckfastleigh is off the A38.
By Rail: Totnes
FACILITIES
Shop, Buffet & Restaurant, Some Provision for Disabled, Car & Coach Parking, Museum, Picnic Area, Model Railway, Devon Cream Tea Services, River Cruise.

Wilson's View
Now in the hands of volunteers, the Dart Valley will once again be serving up Devon cream teas, with the accent on cream - and just a dash of chocolate. Opened in 1969 as a commercial undertaking, the Dart Valley line has had problems in the past but the volunteers have now formed the South Devon Railway Trust to run the line on a voluntary basis. They are confident that, with your custom, they will see a change in fortune for the railway - I wish them every success.

Southport Railway Centre

STANDARD GAUGE

When

13.00 and 17.00 (or dusk) weekends October to April. Daily in June and first week in September.
11.00 and 17.00 weekends June to September. 10.30 and 16.30 daily in July and August.
Train rides every Sunday from June 28th to September 6th and Bank Holidays. Santa trains run every weekend from November 28th to December 20th 10.30 - 16.00.

What

Leap Year Thomas event	February 29th, March 1st.
Four Days of Steam	April 17-20th.
Thomas' Gala Party	August 8-9th.
Enthusiasts Weekend	August 30-31st.
Winter Steam Special	November 1st.
Santa Trains	November 28-29th, December 5,6,12,13,19 and 20th.

Where

LOCATION
Motive Power Depot, Derby Road, Southport PR9 0TY. Telephone (0704)530693.
ACCESS
By Bus: Services to Southport from most parts of the country.
By Road: On A565.
By Rail: Southport 5 minutes walk.
FACILITIES
Shop, Buffet, Car Parking, Provision for Disabled, Steam Hauled Brake Van Rides, Party Hire Train, Children's Specials with Thomas look-alike.

Wilson's View

Steam at the Seaside, the Railway Centre is based in what was once 23C and Ex-L & Y motive power depot. Here lies Sir Cecil Raikes - gone but not forgotten. Sir Cecil is a survivor of almost supernatural proportions. Built for the Mersey Railway in 1885 by Beyer Peacock, sold to the Coppice Colliery in 1903, donated by the NCB to the British Transport Commision in 1956, stored until 1964, (at Crewe if memory serves), Cecil went to Liverpool in 1967 before arriving at Southport in 1979 - he's still there, go and see for yourself.

1990, but it could be 1950 as the great Marquess waits the right away from Bewdley on the Severn Valley Railway. Photo C.D. Wilson

South Tynedale Railway

NARROW GAUGE

When

				A				A
Alston	Dep	11.15	12.00	13.00	14.00	15.00	16.00	17.00
Gilderdale	Arr	11.30	12.15	13.15	14.15	15.15	16.15	17.15
				A				A
Gilderdale	Dep	11.35	12.25	13.25	14.25	15.25	16.25	17.25
Alston	Arr	11.50	12.40	13.40	14.40	15.40	16.40	17.40

Notes:
(A) runs on steam service days only. Steam Haulage runs from Good Friday, all Bank Holidays (Saturday, Sunday and Monday) and every weekend from Spring Bank Holiday to end of September.
Diesel services run on all other operating days.

Service Operates:
April 17-26th. May Saturdays, Sundays and Bank holidays and daily from 23-31st. June daily except on Mondays and Fridays. July to September 6th daily, then Mondays and Fridays excepted to October. Sundays in October. December 6,12,13,20,27 and 28th.

What

Childrens Day	May 27th.
Steam Enthusiasts Weekend	July 25-26th.
Diesel Enthusiasts & Open Day	October 11th.
Santa Trains	December 6,12,13 and 20th.
Mince Pie Specials	December 27-28th.

Where

LOCATION
Alston Station, Alston, Cumbria CA9 3JB. Telephone (0434)381696.
ACCESS
By Bus: Services from Newcastle/Haltwhistle/Keswick to Alston. Bus Link enquiry Tel: 0228 812812
By Road: Alston is at the junction of the A686 & A689. The A686 from Penrith / Haydon Bridge. The A689 from Bishop Auckland/Brampton or the B6277 from Barnard Castle.
By Rail: Haltwhistle, Stanhope (Summer Sundays) bus link, Langwathby also bus linked on certain days.
FACILITIES
Shop, Buffet, Car & Coach Parking, Provision for Disabled, Picnic area, Tourist Information.
FARES
Adult 1.60, Children 5 to 15 half fare, reductions on pre-booked parties(10 +), Dogs 25p. New for 1992 a joint ticket for the railway and the Killhope Wheel Lead Mine (price to be announced).
LOCOS
Henschel 0-4-0T Thomas Edmondson, Chrzanow 0-6-0WT Naklo, Hunslet 0-4-2T Chaka's Kraal No 6. Diesels: Phoenix, Ayle, Naworth. The Peril.

Wilson's View

Not only does this line have some very cosmopolitan motive power, it has some splendid signalling to match. The box at the West end of Alston Station controls all the movements in and around the station, engine sheds and carriage sidings as well as the half barrier level crossing. To keep the scale right, BR shunt signal arms have been used - very effectively. To go with the charming old station at Alston there are smart new carriage works and engine sheds. The STR may not be the most accessible of lines, but the effort of getting there is well worth it.

Steamtown: Carnforth

NARROW GAUGE   STANDARD GAUGE

When
Crag Bank shuttle (standard gauge) Sundays and Bank Holidays, Easter to November. 15inch gauge line runs Saturdays, Sundays and Bank Holidays from Easter to November.

What
During the season there will be a number of special events, see railway press for details.

Where
LOCATION
Steamtown Railway Museum, Warton Road, Carnforth, Lancashire LA5 9HX. Telephone (0524)732100/734220.
ACCESS
By Bus: From Lancaster Ribble or Lancaster City Services to Carnforth.
By Road: Via M6 to Jct 35 then B6254 to town centre then follow signs.
By Rail: Carnforth.
FACILITIES
Shop, Buffet, Collectors Corner, Model Railway, Parking.
FARES
From 1.50 on static display days to 2.80 on main line loco days. Family fares, concessions for children, O.A.P.'s and parties.

Wilson's View
If I were presenting prizes for the best comeback in recent years, Steamtown would be a very strong contender. The place has been brought back from the brink by a whole series of events and visiting mainline stars. The site itself has also undergone a good Spring clean, the turntable has been put back in action and work is ongoing to repair the Cenotaph Coaling Plant. If present trends continue, Carnforth will be well worth more than a `Brief Encounter'.

Strathspey Railway

STANDARD GAUGE

When
Table A

	D				X	EX	EX	EX
Aviemore Dep	11.00	12.20	14.10	15.40	16.50	18.30	20.50	22.00
B of Garten Arr	11.20	12.40	14.30	16.00	17.10	18.50	21.10	22.20
					X	EX	EX	EX
B of Garten Dep	10.30	11.40	13.00	15.00	16.20	18.00	20.20	21.30
Aviemore Arr	10.50	12.00	13.20	15.20	16.40	18.20	20.40	21.50

D: Diesel hauled Sundays May 31st to August 30th.
X: Saturdays excepted from May 25th to August 31st (does not run Bank Holiday Saturday).
EX: Wednesday only July 1st to August 26th.

Service operates
January 1-2nd. March 28-29th. April 1,5,8,12-26 and 29th. May 3,4,6,10,13,17 and 20th then daily from 23rd to September 5th. September 6-30th except Saturday 5,12 and 19th. October 4,7,11,14,18,21,25 and 28th. December 19, 20, 26, 27 and 31st.

What

Members Day	March 28th.
Mad March	March 29th (Adults at child fares).
Boat of Garten Beer Fest	May 23-24th.
Thomas Weekend	September 26-27th (provisional)
Santa Trains	December 19-20th.
Hogmanay Special	December 31st with 01.00 service on 1.1.93

Where

LOCATION
The Station, Boat of Garten, Inverness-shire PH24 3BH
(Main Station is Aviemore).
Telephone (047983)692.
ACCESS
By Bus: Express services from major towns to Aviemore, Highland services to Aviemore.
By Road: Aviemore is on A9.
By Rail: Aviemore.
FACILITIES
Shop, Buffet, Museum(Boat of Garten), Some Provision for Disabled, Wine & Dine
Service(Booking essential phone (047983) 258), Car & Coach Parking.
LOCOS
Ex-LMS 4-6-0 5025, 0-6-0ST Victor, 0-6-0ST No60, D5394.
FARES
Adult 1st class 5.00, Adult 3rd class 3.60, Family 3rd class 9.60 (2 adults & up to 2 children),
other children half fare.

Wilson's View

Aviemore to Boat of Garten on what was the Highland Railway's Aviemore-Forres route,
once the mainline from Perth to Inverness. Strathspey are also the hosts to a splendid old
Caley goods engine, the McIntosh 812 class 0-6-0 No.CR 828, which should be in action this
year. Keeping 828 company is another oddity - a Bagnall 0-6-0ST with outside Walschaerts
motion. In years gone by, 60009 ran at Strathspey - will she again?

Swanage Railway

STANDARD GAUGE

The Purbeck Line

When

Table A

		DY	X					X	DY
Swanage	Dep	10.00	11.00	12.10	13.20	14.30	15.40	16.50	18.00
Herston Halt		10.05	11.05	12.15	13.25	14.35	15.45	16.55	18.05
Harmans X	Arr	10.15	11.15	12.25	13.35	14.45	15.55	17.05	18.15
Harmans X	Dep	10.20	11.30	12.40	13.50	15.00	16.10	17.20	18.20
Herston Halt		10.30	11.40	12.50	14.00	15.10	16.20	17.30	18.30
Swanage	Arr	10.35	11.45	12.55	14.05	15.15	16.25	17.35	18.35

Table B

		D							D	D	D
Swanage	Dep	10.00	11.00	12.10	13.20	14.30	15.40	16.50	19.00	20.00	22.00
Herston		10.05	11.05	12.15	13.25	14.35	15.45	16.55	19.05	20.05	22.05
Harmans X	Arr	10.15	11.15	12.25	13.35	14.45	15.55	17.05	19.15	20.15	22.15
Harmans X	Dep	10.20	11.30	12.40	13.50	15.00	16.10	17.20	19.20	20.20	22.20
Herston Halt		10.28	11.40	12.50	14.00	15.10	16.20	17.30	19.30	20.30	22.30
Swanage	Arr	10.33	11.45	12.55	14.05	15.15	16.25	17.35	19.35	20.35	22.35

Services Operate:

Table A: January 1-5,12,19 and 26th. February 2,16 and 22nd. March 1,7,14,15,21,22,28 and 29th. April 4,5,11,12 and 17-26th. May 2,7,9,10,14,16,17 and 21-31st. June daily (except 21st). July daily (except 12,26 and 28th). August Friday to Monday (except 30-31st). September 4-27th. October 3,4,10,11,17,18,24 and 26-31st. November 7,8,14,15,21 and 22nd. December 26th to January 3rd 1993.

Table B: February 8,9 and 23rd. May 3-4th. June 21st. July 12,26 and 28-30th. Tuesdays, Wednesdays and Thursdays August 4th to September 3rd. September 13th. October 25th. November 1st.

Notes: (D) Diesel hauled. (X) Commences April 4th and does not run after September 27th (runs March 15th). (Y) Runs May 23-31st. June 7,14 and 28th. July 5.11.13-24,27 and 31st. August 1-29th (Friday to Monday). September 4-11th.

What

Photographic Weekend	February 8-9th.
Thomas Weekend	February 22-23rd.
Teddy Bear Special	March 15th.
Mothers Day	March 29th (free gift for Mums).
Hot X Bun Day	April 17th (free Hot X Buns).
Easter Egg Special	April 19-20th (free cream egg for kids)
Vintage Transport Rally	May 3-4th.
Steam Open Day	May 16-17th (everything on display).
Victorian Weekend	June 20-21st.
Dorset Weekend	July 11-12th.
Thomas Weekend	July 25-26th.
Eddie Echo Weekend	August 1-2nd.
Grand Steam Gala	September 12-13th (all locos in steam).
Thomas Week	October 24 to November 1st (with the Fat Controller)
Santa Service	December 5,6,12,13 and 19-24th (booking essential)

Where

LOCATION
The Station, Swanage, Dorset BH19 1HB. Telephone (0929) 425800/425053
ACCESS
By Bus: Wilts & Dorset services from Bournemouth Poole or Wareham.
By Road: Via A351 Wareham/Swanage Road.
By Rail: Wareham.
FACILITIES
Shop, Buffet, Car & Coach Parking, Wine & Dine Service (booking essential), Children's Party Service, Provision for Disabled, Exhibition Coach.
LOCOS
LMS 1F 41708, Ex-Turkish 8F 45160, Industrial 0-6-0, possibly M7 30053, and 257 Squadron, visiting locos to be arranged.
FARES
Adults 3.90, Children 5-15 1.95. Family 9.95. Day Rover 5.00. 5-day ticket 14.00.

Wilson's View

Following management problems in 1991, the Swanage Railway is now back in the control of the volunteers. It is also back to Corfe Castle and that too caused difficulties as it could not be opened to traffic until the Norden 'Park and Ride' facility was ready. Troubles apart, the Swanage Railway has a lovely route and has benefited from a variety of visiting locos and from being the base from which Clive Groome gives his advanced level tuition on his Footplate Ways Courses. Swanage is one to watch; there will be many new and interesting developments to come.

Steam on the Mainline Flying Scotsman Services
in conjunction with SLOA & BR.

For details of steam-hauled passenger trains on BR lines, contact:
FLYING SCOTSMAN SERVICES at Steamtown, Warton Road, Carnforth, Lancs. LA5 9HX
Telephone: 0524 734220   Evenings: 0706 620444 (1800-2100hrs)
ACCESS   VISA

Swindon G.W.R. Museum

STANDARD GAUGE

When
Weekends 10.00-17.00, Sundays 14.00-17.00. Closed Good Friday, Christmas & Boxing Day.

What
Various events and exhibitions related to th Great Western Railway.

Where
LOCATION
G.W.R. Museum, Farringdon Road, Swindon, Wiltshire. Telephone (0793) 526161.
ACCESS
By Bus: Thamesdown Transport.
By Road: Swindon is off junctions 15 or 16 of M4 or on the A420 and A419.
By Rail: Swindon.
FACILITIES
Shop, Street Parking, Possibly joint ticket with N.R.M. on Tour.

Wilson's View
A celebration of the Great Western in photograph, print and artefact. Home of the replica North Star, a 2-2-2 Broad Gauge engine of 1837 vintage. The replica was built utilising some parts from the original locomotive.

Swindon & Cricklade Railway

STANDARD GAUGE

When
Open every weekend with steam service operating from 12.00 to 17.00 at 30 minute intervals. Runs January 1st. April 19-20th. May 24-25th. June 27-28th. September 5-6th. October 31st. November 1st.December 5,6,12,13,19 and 20th.

What
Mince Pie Specials	January 1st, 1992 & 1993
Easter Bunny	April 19-20th.
Thomas Weekend	May 24-25th.
Teddy Bears Picnic	September 5-6th.
Ghost Train	October 31st (evening 9.30).
Winter Steam	November 1st.
Santa Trains	December 5,6,12,13,19 and 20th.

Where
LOCATION
Blunsdon Station, Tadpole Lane, Blunsdon, Nr Swindon. Telephone (0793)771615.
ACCESS
By Bus: Thamesdown Transport from Swindon.
By Road: Blunsdon is off A419, 3 miles west of Swindon signposted Purton.
By Rail: Swindon.
FACILITIES
Shop, Buffet, Car & Coach Parking, Some Provision for Disabled , Museum Coach, Collectors Corner, Signal Box Access, Children's Party and Group Visits Service.
LOCOS
Peckett 0-4-0 Merlin, Barclay 0-4-0 Richard Trevithick.

Wilson's View
This line was built by the Midland & South Western Junction Railway to link Andover on the London & South Western with Andoversford on the Great Western's line between Cheltenham and Kingham. Today, the SCR occupy the section between Blunsdon and Cricklade, the Society's headquarters being at Blunsdon along with the stock and a nicely refurbished country railway station.

Talyllyn Railway

NARROW GAUGE

When
Table A

		A	B	C	D	A	E	F	G	A	V
Tywyn (Wharf)	Dep	10.00	10.20	10.25	10.35	11.20	11.25	11.30	11.40	11.50	12.25
Dolgoch Falls		10.30	10.50	10.55	11.05	11.52	11.55	12.00	12.10	12.22	12.55
Abergynolwyn		10.44	11.04	11.09	11.19	12.06	12.09	12.14	12.24	12.36	13.09
Nant Gwernol	Arr	10.52	11.11	11.16	11.26	12.13	12.16	12.21	12.31	12.43	13.16

		A	B	C	D	A	E	F	G	A	V
Nant Gwernol	Dep	11.00	11.20	11.25	11.35	12.20	12.25	12.30	12.40	13.00	13.40
Abergynolwen	Arr	11.05	11.25	11.30	11.40	12.25	12.30	12.35	12.45	13.05	13.45
Abergynolwen	Dep	11.15	11.55	12.00	12.10	12.45	12.55	13.15	13.15	13.35	14.18
Dolgoch Falls		11.28	12.08	12.13	12.23	12.55	13.08	13.28	13.28	13.45	14.31
Tywyn (Wharf)	Arr	11.58	12.38	12.43	12.53	13.25	13.38	13.58	13.58	14.15	15.03

		VA	B	C	A	E	H	A	B+	J	S
Tywyn (Wharf)	Dep	12.45	13.00	13.20	13.35	14.05	14.25	15.15	15.40	16.05	19.00
Dolgoch Falls		13.15	13.32	13.52	14.08	14.35	14.55	15.48	16.12	16.37	19.30
Abergynolwen		13.29	13.44	14.04	14.21	14.49	15.09	16.01	16.39*	17.04#	19.44
Nant Gwernol	Arr	13.36	13.51	14.11	14.28	14.56	15.16	16.08	16.46	17.11	19.51

		A	B	VA	A	E	H	A	B+	J	S
Nant Gwernol	Dep	13.50	14.00	14.20	14.40	15.05	15.25	16.20	16.57	17.22	20.00
Abergynolwen	Arr	13.55	14.05	14.25	14.45	15.10	15.30	16.25	17.02	17.27	20.05
Abergynolwen	Dep	14.25	14.35	14.55	15.15	15.35	16.00	16.55	17.05	17.30	20.55
Dolgoch Falls		14.35	14.48	15.08	15.25	15.48	16.13	17.08	17.18	17.43	21.10
Tywyn (Wharf)	Arr	15.05	15.18	15.38	15.55	16.18	16.43	17.38	17.48	18.13	21.44

Notes:
A: Monday to Friday, July 18th to September 6th, May 24-29th.
B(+): April 17-24th or April 19-21st only.
C: Monday to Friday, May 30th to July 17th, September 7-25th.
D: Sunday only July 18th to September 6th.
E: Daily, April 6th to May 10th.
F: Monday to Friday, May 11-22nd, May 30th to July 17th, September 7th to October 31st.
G: Saturdays and Sundays only, May 11th to October 31st.
H: Daily May 11th to October 31st (departs 15.30 Monday to Friday, July 18th to September 6th and May 24-29th. On the Nant Gwernol - Tywyn service.
J: Monday to Friday only, May 30th to July 17th. Then daily to September 11th.
S: Special evening service Sundays only, July 19th to August 30th.
V: Vintage trains Saturdays only July 18th to September 6th, except August 15th.
VA: Saturdays only Vintage trains, May 30th to July 17th and September 7-25th.
* Arrives 16.49. # Arrives 16.24.

What
Special services on Saturday August 15th, phone for details. Other special events during the year see press for details.

Where
LOCATION
Talyllyn Railway, Wharfe Station, Tywyn, Gwynedd LL36 9EY. Telephone (0654) 710472
ACCESS
By Bus: BWS Gwynedd services to Tywyn.
By Road: On A493 Barmouth/Machynlleth Road.
By Rail: Tywyn (300 yds away).
FACILITIES
Shop, Buffet, Museum, Car & Coach Parking, Some Provision for Disabled,
Picnic Area Dolgoch Falls (Dolgoch Station).
LOCOS
0-4-0WT No2 Dolgoch, 0-4-2ST No3 Sir Haydn, 0-4-2ST No2 Edward Thomas, 0-4-2T No7 Tom Rolt, 0-4-0WT No6 Douglas, 0-4-2ST No1 Talyllyn.

Wilson's View

For more than forty years, the Talyllyn has been an example to the railway preservation movement. The Talyllyn proved it could be done and hundreds of others have emulated them. Sadly, not all the original TR rescuers are alive today, but the railway they helped to rescue is still a delight to the thousands who visit. Some of the railway's charm is undoubtedly provided by mother nature, but more than a fair share is produced by the splendid coaching stock and locomotives, ably assisted by a very professional group of volunteers.

Tanfield Railway

STANDARD GAUGE

When

Service operates every Sunday and Bank Holiday Monday from Easter to December. Thursdays & Saturdays in June , July and August.

Sunniside	Dep	11.42	13.12	14.12	15.12	16.12	
Andrews House	Arr	11.47	13.17	14.17	15.17	16.17	
Andrews House	Dep	11.48	13.18	14.18	15.18	16.18	
Causey Arch	Arr	11.55	13.25	14.25	15.25	16.25	
East Tanfield	Trains will run to this station as soon as possible						
Causey Arch	Dep		12.08	13.38	14.38	15.38	16.38
Andrews House	Arr		12.15	13.45	14.45	15.45	16.45
Andrews House	Dep	11.30	13.00	14.00	15.00	16.00	
Sunniside	Arr	11.35	13.05	14.05	15.05	16.05	

Notes: The 16.00 ex-Andrews House may not run in winter. Extra services will run on Bank Holidays and peak summer times.

What

Gala Weekends   Spring & August Bank Holidays

Where

LOCATION
The Tanfield Railway, Old Marley Hill, Sunniside, Gateshead, Tyne and Wear. Postal address: 33 Stocksfield Avenue, Newcastle-upon-Tyne NE5 2DX. Telephone (091) 2742002.
ACCESS
By Bus: From Newcastle or Gateshead X30 Monday-Saturday, X75 Summer Sundays, and any bus to Sunniside on winter Sundays.
By Road: Off A6076 Sunniside to Stanley road.
By Rail: Newcastle-upon-Tyne.
FACILITIES
Shop, Buffet, Car & Coach Parking, Some Provision for Disabled.
LOCOS
Irwell, Progress, Sir Cecil A.Cochrane, Wellington, No2 and No21. All these locos are intended to be in steam on Gala days with a selection operating on other working days.

Wilson's View

The 'Marsden Rattler' rides again, or at least the Causey Rambler does - and they could be twins. The recreation of a colliery railway passenger service has been the theme at Tanfield, and they have succeeded. Four-and six-wheel wooden coaches, diminutive industrial locos, a half-round engine shed, stone built halts with cinder platforms. The newly-opened Causey Arch section gives access to the famous arch itself, which was constructed using methods imported by the Romans! Tanfield may not have any mainline giants, but it lacks nothing in atmosphere!

Teifi Valley Railway

When
Service operates daily from Good Friday to October, 11.00 to 17.00
Steam Haulage Sundays and Wednesdays in peak season only.

What
Easter Sunday Fair	April 19th
Dragon Day	Mid August (Date to be confirmed).
Victorian Day	End August (Date to be confirmed).
Santa Trains run from	December 21st to 23rd.

Where
LOCATION
Teifi Valley Railway, Henllan Station Yard, Llandysul, Dyfed SA44 5TD. Telephone (0559) 371077
ACCESS
By Road: Henllan is just off the A475 Cardigan to Lampeter road, or the A484 Cardigan to Carmarthen road.
By Rail: Carmarthen (16 miles).
FACILITIES
Shop, Buffet, Picnic Area, Woodland Walks, Open-air Theatre, Children's Steam Loco Alan George, Diesels Sammy and Sholto.
FARES
Adults 3.00, Children 1.50

Wilson's View
A narrow gauge line which concentrates its efforts on the family market rather than the enthusiast. In addition to the railway, there are picnic sites and nature trails and for good measure an open air theatre.

Ex-LMS Jubilee 4-6-0 5593 heads a lunch express towards Leicester North.

Vale of Rheidol Railway

NARROW GAUGE

When

		X	Y	X	Y	X	Y
Aberystwyth	Dep	10.45	11.00	12.15	14.00	14.30	15.45
		X	Y	X	Y	X	Y
Devils Bridge	Dep	12.30	13.00	14.15	16.00	16.30	17.30

Notes:
X runs daily from May 25th to 29th. July 13th to September 4th Monday to Friday only.
Y runs daily from April 17th to May 24th, and May 30th to July 12th.July 18th to August 30th
Saturdays & Sundays only. Daily September 5th to October 4th.

Service operates:
April 17th to October 4th. Single journey time 1 hour, return journey time 3 hours.

Where

LOCATION
The Locomotive Shed, Park Avenue, Aberystwyth, Dyfed SY23 1PG. Telephone (0970) 625819
during operating season, (0970) 615993 at other times.
ACCESS
By Bus: Crossville service to Aberystwyth.
By Road: Aberystwyth is on the junction of the A487 and the A4120.
By Rail: Aberystwyth (adjacent).
FACILITIES
Shop, Buffet, Car & Coach parking.
LOCOS
7,8,9 and 10, purpose built for VOR by GWR and Davies Metcalf.
FARES
Adults 9.40, Children 1.00 per child with each adult paying full fare. Other children 4.70.

Wilson's View

Once the last outpost of steam on British Rail, this one foot eleven and a half inch gauge line,
which opened ninety years ago in 1902, is now under the same management as the Brecon
Mountain Railway. However, this line has seen numerous other ownerships. It was
absorbed into the Cambrian Railway in 1913, the GWR acquired it in 1923, in 1948 it
became part of the Western Region, and in 1963 it was transferred to the Midland Region.
Between 1967 and 1980, the line was covered by the BR corporate image of Blue with the
arrows totem, it then reverted to a more character image with a mix of GWR and V.o R.
liveries. Today, the livery is a mix of Cambrian and Brecon - the scenery is pretty good too!

TENTERDEN

Wells Harbour Railway

When

Table A

Wells	Dep	10.50	11.30	12.10	12.50	13.25	14.30	15.10	15.50	16.30	17.10
Pinewoods	Dep	10.30	11.10	11.50	12.30	13.10	14.10	14.50	15.30	16.10	16.50	17.30

Service operates:
Easter week then weekends only until Spring Bank Holiday. Daily from Spring Bank Holiday to July, and from September 1st to mid-September. Then weekends only to end of October.

Table B

Wells	Dep	10.10	10.50	11.30	12.10	12.50	13.30	14.10	14.50
		15.30	16.10	16.50	17.30	18.10	18.50	19.50	
Pinewoods	Dep	09.50	10.30	11.10	11.50	12.30	13.10	13.50	14.30
		15.10	15.50	16.30	17.10	17.50	18.30	19.30	

Service operates:
Daily from July to September. At peak times during mid-July to end of August services run at 15 minute intervals. Service operates late evenings in high season.

Notes: On Table B the last departure from Wells Harbour is 23.10 and 22.45 on Sundays. Services between 19.30 and 23.10 are advertised locally and are according to demand.

What
Longest operational day of any minimum gauge railway.

Where
LOCATION
Beach Road, Wells-Next-the-Sea, Norfolk.
ACCESS
By Bus: Eastern Counties service to Wells.
By Road: On the A149, Beach Road is by the quay.
By Rail: Sheringham.
FACILITIES
Public transport from Pinewoods Caravan/Camp site to Wells Harbour and the beach.

Wilson's View
A privately owned railway connecting a major camp-site with the town and harbour, this line has the longest operating day of any comparable system and certainly the longest for a ten and a quarter inch railway. Wells must be something of a mecca for minimum gauge fans, as the town also boasts a minimum gauge railway to the nearby shrine at Walsingham.

Wells & Walsingham Railway

When

Table 1

Operates daily Easter weekend then Spring Bank Holiday to mid-September.

Wells	Dep	10.00	11.20	12.40	14.00	15.20	16.40
Warham St Mary		R	R	R	R	R	R
Wighton		R	R	R	R	R	R
Walsingham	Arr	10.25	11.45	13.05	14.25	15.45	17.05
Walsingham	Dep	10.40	12.00	13.20	14.40	16.00	17.20
Wighton		R	R	R	R	R	R
Warham St Mary		R	R	R	R	R	R
Wells	Arr	11.05	12.25	13.45	15.05	16.25	17.45

Table 2

Operates daily from Easter Tuesday to Spring Bank Holiday then mid September to September 30th.

Wells	Dep	10.30	12.00	14.00	15.30
Warham St Mary		R	R	R	R
Wighton		R	R	R	R
Walsingham	Arr	10.55	12.25	14.25	15.55
Walsingham	Dep	11.15	12.45	14.45	16.15
Wighton		R	R	R	R
Warham St Mary		R	R	R	R
Wells	Arr	11.40	13.10	15.10	16.40

*R: Request stop only.

What

Evening charter train hire (booking essential).

Where

LOCATION
Wells & Walsingham Railway, Stiffkey Road, Wells-Next-the-Sea, Norfolk.
ACCESS
By Bus: Eastern Counties service to Wells.
By Road: On the A149 at junction of B1105.
By Rail: Sheringham
FACILITIES
Shop, Buffet (in restored signalbox), Car Parking.
LOCOS
Garratt specially built for the line.

Wilson's View

Wells worth a pilgrimage, if minimum gauge is your idea of a pun! This is Britain's longest ten and a quarter inch gauge line. The line links the old Norfolk town of Walsingham with the seaside at Wells, and the whole line more or less owes its existence to Captain Francis. Motive power is the unique purpose-built Garrett.

Welsh Highland Railway

When

Porthmadog Dep   10.30A 11.15A 12.00   12.45B 13.30   14.15   15.00   15.45   16.30

Steam service operates:

April	18th - 26th
May	2-4th,9,10,16,17,23rd-31st.
June	Every Saturday and Sunday
July	Saturdays and Sundays and 28th to 31st.
August	Daily except Mondays & Fridays. Bank Holiday Monday.
September	1 - 3rd. and every Saturday & Sunday.

Diesel service operates:

April	17th
May	5 - 8th then Tuesday, Thursday & Friday from 12th to 22nd
June	Tuesday to Friday
July	Monday to Friday from 1st to 24th and 27th and 31st.
August	Monday and Friday except Bank Holiday Monday
September	4th, then Tuesday to Thursday until 24th.
October	17th to 25th.

Notes:

(A) does not run April 17th, 21-26th, May 9,10,16,17th and 26-30th. June 6,7,13,14,20,21,27 and 28th. September 5.6.12.13.19.20.26 and 27th. October 17-25th.
(B) This service operates on dates when (A) is not running. Russel or Gelert will normally haul steam services. Glaslyn will haul diesel services. Extra services may run as required and at special events.

What

Special events during the year, see press for details.

Where

LOCATION
Welsh Highland Railway, Gelerts Farm Works, Madoc Street West, Porthmadog, Gwynedd LL49 9DY. Telephone (0766) 513402
ACCESS
By Bus: BWS Gwynedd services from major towns to Porthmadog.
By Road: Porthmadog is on junction of A487 and A497
By Rail: Porthmadog
FACILITIES
Shop, Buffet, Car & Coach Parking, Track Bed Walk from Pen-y-mount.
LOCOS
Ex-WHR 2-6-2T Russell, 0-4-2T Bagnall Gelert Ruston, Hornsby 4WDM No 10 Glaslyn.

Wilson's View

The Welsh Highland have a new attraction for this season, the newly restored Bagnall 0-4-2T, now named Bedggelert. This handsome loco will join the much admired Hunslet 2-6-2T Russell (he of the huge brass dome), and Karen the 0-4-2T built by Peckett during 1942. Karen went to the Welsh Highland via the Selukwe Peak Light Railway of Southern Rhodesia - some journey!

Welshpool & Llanfair Light Railway

When

Table A

Llanfair Caereinion	Dep	10.45	13.45	16.15
Castle Caereinion	Dep	11.10	14.10	16.40
Welshpool (Raven Sq)	Arr	11.35	14.35	17.05
Welshpool	Dep	12.00	15.00	17.15
Castle Caereinion	Dep	12.25	15.20	17.35
Llanfair Caereinion	Arr	12.50	15.50	18.05

Trains also call on request at Heniarth, Cyfronydd and Sylfaen.

Service Operates:
Daily April 17-26th, May 26-31st and July 17th to September 6th. Saturday & Sunday May 2-23rd, June 6-14th and September 19th to October 4th. Daily (except Monday & Friday) June 16th to July 16th and September 8-17th.

Table B

Llanfair Caereinion	Dep	10.45	11.45	13.30	14.50	16.15	18.30
Castle Caereinion	Dep	11.10	12.10	13.55	15.15	16.40	18.55
Welshpool	Arr	11.35	12.35	14.20	15.40	17.05	19.20
Welshpool	Dep	12.00	13.45	15.05	16.30	17.15	19.39
Castle Caereinion	Dep	12.20	14.05	15.25	16.50	17.35	19.50
Llanfair Caereinion	Arr	12.50	14.35	15.55	17.20	18.05	20.20

Service operates:
Spring Bank Holiday Sunday & Monday, August Bank Holiday Sunday & Monday and every Sunday in August.

What

Friends of Thomas run June 20-21st. Steam Gala September 5-6th (both special timetables). Santa Trains in December, dates to be announced.

Where

LOCATION
Llanfair Caereinion Station, Llanfair Caereinion, Welshpool, Powys. Telephone (0938) 810441
ACCESS
By Bus: Crossville service from Shrewsbury, Oswestry and Newtown to Welshpool.
By Road: Welshpool is on junction of A458 and A490. Llanfair Caereinion is on the A458, ten miles west of Welshpool.
By Rail: Welshpool
FACILITIES
Shop, Buffet, Car & Coach Parking, Restaurant (Raven Inn at the Welshpool Raven Sq Station).
FARES
Adult return 5.80, Single 3.90, Family 14.00.
LOCOS
0-6-0T No2 Countess, 0-4-0T No8 Dougal, 0-8-0T No10 Sir Drefaldwyn, 0-6-2T No12 Joan and 2-6-2T No85.

Wilson's View

This two foot six gauge line has a ferocious mile-long climb at 1:29 - Golfa bank. It also has one of the smallest two foot six gauge locos in the country, the diminutive Dougal. Dougal is ex-Provan Gas Works, and weighs in at just six tons ten hundredweight. The eight mile long line's other claims to fame are the diverse collection of locomotives and rolling stock which come from sources as far apart as Austria and Antigua.

West Somerset Railway

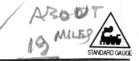

When
Table A (off peak)

		S	D	S	D
Minehead	Dep	10.15	12.15	14.30	16.55
Dunster(R)		10.21	12.21	14.36	17.01
Blue Anchor		10.30	12.27	14.45	17.14
Washford		10.39	12.35	14.54	17.22
Watchet		10.48	12.43	15.02	17.30
Doniford Beach		10.52	12.47	15.06	17.34
Williton	Arr	10.56	12.49	15.09	17.36
Williton	Dep	11.05	12.53	15.13	17.37
Stogumber(R)		11.16	13.03	15.26	17.47
Crowcombe(R)		11.25	13.10	15.37	17.54
Bishops Lydeard	Arr	11.35	13.19	15.47	18.03

		D	S	D	S
Bishops Lydeard	Dep	10.30	12.15	14.45	16.10
Crowcombe(R)		10.40	12.30	14.55	16.25
Stogumber(R)		10.47	12.39	15.02	16.34
Williton	Arr	10.56	12.48	15.11	16.43
Williton	Dep	10.58	12.52	15.12	16.46
Doniford Beach		11.01	12.56	15.15	16.50
Watchet		11.05	13.00	15.19	16.54
Washford		11.13	13.09	15.27	17.03
Blue Anchor		11.21	13.17	15.35	17.11
Dunster(R)		11.27	13.24	15.41	17.18
Minehead	Arr	11.32	13.30	15.46	17.24

Service Operates:
March 14,15,21 and 22nd. April 4,5,11,12,15-17,21-26 and 28-30th. May 5-7,9,10,12-14,16,17,19-21,30 and 31st. June 1-30th. July 1-17th. September 14-25, 29 and 30th. October 1,3,4,6-8,10,11,13-15,17,18,20-22,24 and 25th.

Table B (peak)

Minehead	Dep	10.15	12.10	14.00	15.45	17.30
Dunster (R)		10.21	12.16	14.06	15.51	17.36
Blue Anchor		10.30	12.25	14.15	16.00	17.45
Washford		10.39	12.34	14.24	16.09	17.54
Watchet		10.47	12.42	14.32	16.17	18.02
Doniford Beach		10.51	12.46	14.36	16.21	18.06
Williton	Arr	10.56	12.51	14.41	16.26	18.11
Williton	Dep	11.01	12.56	14.46	16.31	18.16
Stogumber		11.14	13.09	14.59	16.44	18.29
Crocombe		11.25	13.20	15.10	16.55	18.40
Bishops Lydeard	Arr	11.35	13.30	15.20	17.05	18.50

Bishops Lydeard	Dep	10.25	12.20	14.10	15.55	17.40
Crowcombe (R)		10.40	12.35	14.25	16.10	17.55
Stogumber (R)		10.49	12.44	14.34	16.19	18.04
Williton	Arr	10.58	12.53	14.43	16.28	18.13
Williton	Dep	11.03	12.57	14.47	16.32	18.17
Doniford Beach (R)		11.07	13.01	14.51	16.36	18.21
Watchet		11.11	13.05	14.55	16.40	18.25
Washford		11.20	13.14	15.04	16.49	18.34
Blue Anchor		11.28	13.22	15.12	16.57	18.42
Dunster(R)		11.35	13.29	15.19	17.00	18.49
Minehead	Arr	11.41	13.35	15.25	17.10	18.55

Service Operates:

April 18-20th. May 23-29th. July 18th to September 13th. Special services and timetables will be in force on March 28 & 29th, May 2-4th, September 26 & 27th and October 31st.

Notes:

S and D refer to steam or diesel traction. There are bus connections to and from Taunton with trains at Bishops Lydeard. On the off-peak service the buses depart Taunton Castle way at 11.15 and 15.35 calling at Taunton BR at 11.20 and 15.40. Buses leave Bishops Lydeard for Taunton at 11.45 and 16.25.
Peak service times are: Depart Taunton 09.35 (WSO) 11.35, 13.15, 15.05 (SO) 16.55. Depart from Bishops Lydeard at 12.05, 13.55 (SO), 15.45 (SO) 17.30, 18.55 (WSO).
(WSO) Wednesday & Saturday only (SO) Saturday only.

What

Diesel Weekend	March 28-29th and October 31st.
Vintage Weekend	August 1-2nd.
Spring Steam	May 2-4th.
Taunton Rail 150	July 4-5th.
Autumn Steam	September 26-27th.

Special timetables apply on above weekend services.

Where

LOCATION
The Railway Station, Minehead, Somerset TA24 5BG. Telephone (0643) 4996.
ACCESS
By Bus: Special services link Taunton BR with Bishops Lydeard. At other times Southern National services from Taunton pass close to Bishops Lydeard and serve Minehead.
By Road: Minehead is on A39, Bishops Lydeard is on A358 Taunton to Williton road.
By Rail: Taunton (through fares available).
FACILITIES
Shop, Buffet, Car & Coach Parking, Museums (GWR at Blue Anchor, SDJR at Washford), Picnic Sites (Crowcombe and Stogumber), Provision for Disabled, Wine & Dine Service (booking essential).
LOCOS
Ex-S&DJR 7F 53808, ex-GWR 0-6-0PT 6412, Ex-GWR 0-6-0 3205, Ex-GWR 2-6-2T 4561 plus visiting locos to be announced.
FARES
Minehead to Bishops Lydeard return: Adults 6.00 Children 3.00 Family 15.00 (2 Adults & 2 Children)
* Rates for guidance only. 1992 fares not advised.

Wilson's View   LENGTH

The longest line in Britain gives the traveller views of the coast and the Quantocks as it rolls through such delightfully named spots as Blue Anchor Bay and Stogumber, en-route from Minehead to Bishops Lydeard - anyone know what a Bishops Lydeard is? answers on a postcard please! The line also offers some equally tasty motive power with a Collett 0-6-0 3205, S&D 2-8-0 53808 ably supported by the small Prairie 4561 and Pannier 6412. The real highlight of the WSR's year is the week-long Gala, usually held during the first week of September.

Winchcombe Railway Museum

MINIMUM GAUGE

When
Daily from Easter to end of October, weekends and holidays November to March, 13.30 to 18.00 (or dusk). Closed Christmas Day.

What
Special exhibitions throughout the year (phone for details).

Where
LOCATION
23 Gloucester Street, Winchcombe, Gloucestershire GL54 5LX. Telephone (0242) 620641 or 602257.
ACCESS
By Bus: Castleways service from Cheltenham.
By Road: On the B4632 Cheltenham to Stratford-on-Avon road (old A46).
By Rail: Cheltenham (8 miles).
FACILITIES
Shop, Buffet, Picnic Area, Pets Corner, Play Area, Provision for Disabled, Evening group visits, Barbeque Facilities, Party rates for 8 or more, Extensive collection of Lineside Notices, Historically accurate reconstruction of medieval herb garden, Private inspections by prior arrangement.
FARES
Adults 1.60, OAP 1.25, Accompanied Children 50 pence.
LOCOS
Not applicable, though there is a garden railway.

Wilson's View
Alight from the GWR at Winchcombe and wander along to this remarkable small exhibits museum. Every aspect of trackside ironwork is on display in a garden noted more for its Block Bells than Bluebells. There are too many examples of railway signalling and trackside notices to list - you'll just have to check them out for yourself.

Paddlesteamer Waverley

When
Sailings from Easter to mid-October.

When

Paddlesteamer Waverley
In April, May and June sailings on the Clyde and to the Western Isles, Northern Ireland, North West England and the Bristol Channel.
Late June, July and August sailings take place on the Clyde and from Glasgow, Helensburgh, Dunoon, Rothesay, Largs, Ayr, Tarbet and Campbeltown.
In early September the Waverley cruises the Solent, Southampton, Swanage, Southsea, Sandown and Weymouth.
In late September and early October Waverley sails the Thames and the Sussex, Kent, Essex and Suffolk coasts and river estuaries.
The season's final sailings are in the Bristol Channel.

MV Balmoral
April, May and June sailings in the Bristol Channel, Solent, Thames, and the Sussex, Suffolk, Kent and Essex coasts. Tyne and Firth of Forth.
Late June, July, August and early September sailings on the Bristol Channel.
Mid and late September sailings in North Wales and the Clyde for Glasgow Autumn Holiday Weekend.

Kingswear Castle
River paddlesteamer sailings from Chatham Historical Dockyard and the Thames from May to mid-October, with special cruises for Christmas and the New Year.

What
Both Waverley and Balmoral have combined sailings planned with the West Somerset Railway, the Isle of Wight Railway, Swanage Railway and the Isle of Man Railway.

Where
LOCATION
Waverley Steam Navigation Co Ltd. Gwalia Buildings, Barry Docks, South Glamorgan CF6 6XB. Telephone (0446) 720656.
Actual sailing dates and times are available from Waverley Excursions Ltd. at the above address.

Wilson's View
Whilst not strictly a railway timetable, these details are included because Waverley was a railway vessel and still runs cruises in conjunction with several of our preserved lines - and anyway they asked very nicely if we could include them, so how could I refuse.
So there you have it, the end of this year's views.